My Paris Story

*Living, Loving, and Leaping without
a Net in the City of Light*

THE PARIS WOMEN OF SUCCESS

BALBOA.
PRESS
A DIVISION OF HAY HOUSE

Book Concept and Story Collection by:
Dawn Z Bournand (Fabulously Successful Press)

Cover design by: Olena Yashchuk Codet
Editing by: Jennifer Manson and Dawn Z Bournand
Proofing by: Paul Manson, Karen Arena and Hina Wadhwa
Authors Photos by: Claire Morris Photography
(or as noted from authors' personal collections)

A portion of the proceeds from the sale of this book will be donated to Paris for the Philippines (PFTP).

Balboa Press books may be ordered through booksellers or by contacting:

Balboa Press
A Division of Hay House
1663 Liberty Drive
Bloomington, IN 47403
www.balboapress.com
1 (877) 407-4847

Printed in the United States of America.

ISBN: 978-1-4525-9399-9 (sc)
ISBN: 978-1-4525-9401-9 (hc)
ISBN: 978-1-4525-9400-2 (e)

Library of Congress Control Number: 2014904378

Balboa Press rev. date: 03/26/2014

Rave Reviews for My Paris Story:

"For anyone who has ever imagined a life in France... these real life stories will motivate you to make the dream a reality. Sharing in passionate detail their unique paths to Paris, these friendly ambassadors show us that all it takes to get here is commitment, an open heart, and the courage to take the first step... towards the brilliant City of Lights."
– Kristin Espinasse, www.French-Word-A-Day.com

"We've all had them: a perfect moment when a decision is made that will forever change the course of our life. This brilliant book is filled with stories of those who have answered the call of adventure, given into a nudge of inspiration, and best of all, allowed the passion of life to guide the way."
– Marsh Engle, www.MarshEngle.com Inspiring the Lives of
   Women Worldwide!

"I truly enjoyed reading "My Paris Story: Living, Loving and Leaping with a Net in the City of Lights". The stories capture the essence of journeys of divine courage and powerful inspiration, and the authors provide such a beautiful immersion for me to read their life experiences in Paris. In essence, this is a powerful book of women who fearlessly stepped into their courage, passion, and joie de vivre!"
– Nancy Ferrari, CEO, Nancy Ferrari Media & Mentoring
   www.nancyferrari.com

"Ever imagine what it might be like to re-invent your life? Ever dream of doing it in Paris? Here is a collage of 22 women whose stories answer the most powerful question I know: *What can I create*? Read, be transported, and inspired!"
– Laura Munson, *New York Times* and international best-selling
   author http://www.lauramunson.com and founder of Haven
   Retreats http://www.lauramunson.com/retreats

"The secret to success is to have and to follow a dream, to not limit yourself and to cherish and own your destiny. My Paris Story is an extraordinary collection of inspired and inspirational tales from a group of women who have done just that and share their journeys... truly motivating. "

– Janine Marsh, Member of the British Guild of Travel Writers, Editor - Rédacteur en Chef www.thegoodlifefrance.com

"Through all the difficulties of life and work, these authors' stories are evidence that one of the greatest qualities an entrepreneur can possess is determination."

– Denis Bolomier, Founder and Director ADEBEO, Paris, France

"Dream big. Rip off the rear view mirror and don't look back. This is a book that will change your life and inspire you to achieve your dreams!"

– Tammy Kling, Best-selling author, The Compass, Words, Freedom, CEO- The Writers Group

"An unexpected comfort read with a double dose of inspiration! 22 writers humbly share their stories filled with the challenges they've faced and the decisions they've made to reach their goals which ultimately brought them to Paris. Expatriates and entrepreneurs alike will relate to these stories and will be enlightened as to what can happen when positive steps are made and brave decisions are taken."

– Kevin Knight, Co-founder of Expatriates magazine

"What a wonderful book! I'm inspired by the women who followed their dreams all the way to Paris. Engaging, warm, and delightful, you'll want to be friends with all the women who tell of their journeys here. By the end of it, you'll want *My Paris Story* to be your story!"

– Chellie Campbell, Author, The Wealthy Spirit and Zero to Zillionaire, www.chellie.com

"It's always fascinating to learn what brings so many successful women to Paris, but My Paris Story also reveals the deeper, personal histories that are rarely shared at cocktail parties or networking lunches. An inspiring read."

– Heather Stimmler-Hall, Secrets of Paris (www.secretsofparis.com) and author of "Naughty Paris: A Lady's Guide to the Sexy City

"This wonderful book, part travelogue, part inspirational read, is about taking chances, getting lost, and starting again by women who literally and figuratively - lost and found themselves in arguably the most romantic country in the world."

– Tessa Souter, Downbeat Rising Star vocalist and author of Anything I Can Do You Can Do Better (Vermillion-Radom House)

"A must read if you love the freedom to create, inspire and influence the Paris way of living. This book is a collection of the passions, trials and tribulations of pursuing a goal and dream."

– Derek Kwik, Extreme Athlete, Philanthropist and Author of "The Kwik Fix" & "The Kwik Adventures of Baxter the Brave and Tommy the Salami"

"Life isn't about finding yourself. Life is about creating yourself."

George Bernard Shaw

Contents

Introduction xiii

Chapter 1   Connecting the Dots 1
Dawn Z Bournand

Chapter 2   Closet Guru - Coming Out of the Closet with My
Own Unique Gift 7
Michelle Pozon

Chapter 3   A Joyful Heart Makes a Cheerful Face 14
Mady Mendes

Chapter 4   Paris is a Place to Dream 19
Jennifer Manson

Chapter 5   Paris, Je t'aime 24
Julia Willard

Chapter 6   My Sight Seeking Delight 30
Karen Reb Rudel

Chapter 7   Nothing Ventured, Nothing Gained 36
Lesley Kirk Renaud

Chapter 8   A Year Ago Today 42
Addis Kassegn

Chapter 9   My Soul Mate 48
Alecia Caine

Chapter 10 Paris is a Mirror of You 54
Olena Yashchuk Codet

Chapter 11 Seven Years 60
Rebecca Earley

Chapter 12   Paris Became My Creative Playground.........................67
             Petronela Zainuddin
Chapter 13   From Dream to Reality.. 73
             Geneviève Prono
Chapter 14   The Beginning of a New Life 78
             Françoise Bor De Ley
Chapter 15   A Letter to My Child.. 84
             Sanda Taranu
Chapter 16   Rebirth... 89
             Celine Douay
Chapter 17   The Making of Patricia Parisienne 95
             Patricia Rosas
Chapter 18   Your Passion is Your Gift 101
             Claire Morris
Chapter 19   If I Can Make It There.. 107
             Sabrina Makar
Chapter 20   I was Born in Paris.. 112
             Sonia Hadjadj
Chapter 21   There's Never a Wrong Time 118
             Yulin Lee
Chapter 22   Brave Heart.. 124
             Margot Nightingale

My Favorite Place in Paris 131
About the Authors...141

Introduction

You know that serendipitous moment when an idea pops in your head from out of the blue and you feel it is somehow so right? That is how My Paris Story came to life. It was a lightbulb moment as I was sitting in the second gathering for the Paris Women of Success MeetUp group I created in the Spring of 2013. As the women were introducing themselves I was so touched by the amazing stories and the beauty of each and every woman in the room, I knew I had to find a way to help at least some of them share their stories with the world. The idea of a book that pulled together each woman's inspiring journey was divinely planted in my brain and I ran with it!

I enthusiastically said to the group that it would be wonderful to create a collaborative book together and that I would gather details and send them out to everyone before the next monthly meeting. I had no idea what I was getting myself into, but it felt so right. Françoise Bor De Ley was the first brave soul to say yes to herself and to sharing her message and I love her dearly for that. Her "yes" gave me the spark to bring the project to life.

Summer was on its way and people's minds were on vacation, sunshine, rest and relaxation so admittedly my timing could have been better and yet, one by one the authors began to show up and by the time we reached "La Rentrée" (back to school season in France), My Paris Story was truly taking shape. Paris was the magnificent backdrop for each of our stories and yet each woman's story was uniquely hers in how she used Paris as an inspiration to follow her dreams, to gain new insights or to grow in unexpected, life alteringly beautiful ways.

As the stories began to come in, I would often begin to cry as I read through them because they were so honest, so open and so real. It is a true privilege for me to be able to play a part in helping each of these amazing women share her journey, her dreams and her message.

I believe I can speak for all of the authors when I say that we hope our stories will shine a light on your own dreams and inspire you to live, love and take a leap. You don't have to go to Paris to make things happen, you just have to go to the place within you where your joy is found and then follow that feeling to wherever it may take you!

May you live an inspired, fulfilling and giving life,
Dawn

For more information on the My Paris Story book, the authors and upcoming events: www.myparisstory-thebook.com

CHAPTER 1

Connecting the Dots

Dawn Z Bournand

I chose Paris because I knew it would not be easy. I was coming out of a divorce that had knocked the wind out of me and I was trying to learn to breathe again. Somehow I instinctively knew that smooth and easy was not the medicinal balm I needed. I needed a challenge, something to stretch my wings and push me to new limits. Europe came to mind immediately. It seemed a big enough contrast to my golf club, gated community home in the northern Atlanta suburbs.

At the end of my second year at University, a friend and I had decided we wanted to backpack around Europe for a semester. It was a life-changing trip and an adventure I would recommend for every person to do at least once in her life. London had felt like a second home at that time and so that would seem to be the natural choice for this healing sabbatical I was planning to take; but no, London would be too effortless. I needed a challenge, so it had to be France, a country whose language I barely spoke, a place where I had a few acquaintances but no real ties, and the one country that my backpacking adventures actually left me questioning why so many people loved it.

I booked my ticket to Paris, signed up for a year-long photography course and through amazingly serendipitous events even found roommates all within weeks of deciding I would make the leap across the Atlantic, without much of a safety net.

My mother coined a phrase for me during those early days: a phoenix from the flames. I had been burned by the former life I loved disappearing so suddenly, but Paris was my place of re-birth. I savored the exotic cultural mix, the myriad of sounds, fragrances, colors and tastes and the rich blend of the very, very old with avant-garde new. As I came to know the city, I no longer questioned why people loved it so much, I too had fallen under the spell. The healing process had begun.

The challenge of defining myself anew and having absolutely no pre-conceived ideas coming from the people I met, allowed me to ask and answer questions like: Who am I? What really matters to me? What brings me joy? What legacy do I want to leave behind? Admittedly, not very easy questions to answer but they felt so right in this time of figuring out who I was and what made my soul sing.

Traveling to the land of self-discovery is a journey worth taking, and one I highly recommend. You don't have to cross an ocean to do it - unless you want to, of course. Taking the time to ask yourself deep, introspective questions in an environment where all expectations have been left behind and you can be the you that you want to be, the you you have really known all along that you are, opens up an amazing space for possibility.

There is something that happens when you live in Paris as opposed to being "just" a tourist – Paris becomes a part of you. Well, that is how it happened for me, at least. It was not the grand monuments, the awe-inspiring art or the plethora of gourmet goodies that won me over. I grew to adore the crooked, narrow streets, the gorgeous odors of baguettes or pain au chocolat coming from the nearby *boulangerie*, and the quirky shops that you just happen upon every time you walk the city. Even something as mundane as lugging my laundry to the nearby laundromat, with my dear new friend Alexandra from Switzerland, was a charming and memorable moment.

As my photography course finished and the year was coming to an end, I realized I was not ready to go back home just yet. So I found a job teaching English and that is where destiny stepped in. On my way home from work one night I met my future husband on the metro and that was that. Five short months later we were married. That one year trip has now turned into seventeen years; France has become my adopted home and the country where my three sons, the lights of my life, were born.

It has not been all glorious, dream-like moments, though. As it is everywhere, life here has been filled with extreme highs and lows and all the moments and feelings in between. I have so many emotions tied to this beautiful and elusive place.

Shock: being awakened by my mother's call to tell me that Princess Diana had just died from a horrible car accident that had taken place only a short distance away from where I was living.

Horror: holding my oldest son in my arms when he took what I thought was his last breath as his three week old body gave in to the cruel, rare disease (HUS) that was eating him up.

Elation: thanking the dedicated medical staff and one of the only doctors in the world specialized in HUS for doing everything in their power over two long months to save our son's tiny fragile life and succeeding (I will forever be a proponent for social medicine after that experience!)

Terror: answering the call from my family in Florida as I was crossing the Place des Victoires and hearing them tell me that the World Trade Center had just been attacked and that we were possibly at war; wondering if I would ever see my family in the United States again.

Bliss: watching my three sons grow into healthy, happy, heart-centered young men as they embrace their cultural mix and create friendships on both sides of the Atlantic.

Gratitude: reflecting on the very rich life I have experienced here in France, the people I have met, the experiences I have had, and the feelings I have felt.

My leap has certainly not been uneventful and the wonderful part is that along the way, I have created my own safety net. I was eventually able to build my career in France and became a writer, editor and speaker for the MBA market. Then, a few years ago, I realized there was still something more I wanted and needed to do. After speaking to and working with many women executives around the world, I saw their lack of true fulfillment in the work place and in their lives. It seemed so many people were simply "settling" for what they felt was inevitable or necessary. Helping individuals and groups open up to their potential and expand their possibilities is my passion. Thus, my company Fabulously Successful was born.

At the beginning of 2013 a simple fact caught my attention. All of my clients were living outside of France: Brazil, Tokyo, Toronto, London, Miami... but not a single city in France. Surely, there must be at least a few like-minded women in this country, too, who were interested in creating the life they knew they were meant to live. So, on a whim I created a MeetUp group, called it "Paris Women of Success" and asked women interested in meeting on a monthly basis to share the highs and lows of living a successful life to sign up.

The result has been far greater than I ever could have imagined! After just six months the membership was at 250 women and counting. Each meeting reminds me that we can do magnificent things on our own, yet it is even more powerful when we come together and create. As Margaret Mead said, "Never doubt that a small group of thoughtful, committed citizens can change the world; indeed, it's the only thing that ever has." I have already seen the power of our group through new friendships, partnerships, support and service. It has convinced me once more that we are never given an idea without the means to create that which we have dreamed of.

It is now my goal to take this same energy and message to other parts of the world. I want to empower more women to take their leap and reach for their dreams too. My company is a perfect example of thought + action = reality. I am now paid to do what I love – helping people to create their own fulfilling lives. It is true that I could have launched the same thing most anywhere in the world but I deeply believe Paris is what helped make it all possible. I was pushed to ask those significant questions of myself and to find what truly lit me up. It is not that I would wish for adversity for anyone but I do believe that it can make us stronger, clearer and more determined. Perhaps Steve Jobs sums up my Paris experience best when he said, "You can't connect the dots looking forward; you can only connect them looking backward. So you have to trust that the dots will somehow connect in your future. You have to trust in something — your gut, destiny, life, karma, whatever. This approach has never let me down, and it has made all the difference in my life." So don't try to connect the dots looking forward, move in the direction of what you truly desire and trust that everything will fall beautifully into place. It certainly has for me!

Photo by: Claire Morris

Dawn Z Bournand

Dawn Z Bournand is a business and life coach, speaker, author and radio show host working with clients around the world to help them create a business and lifestyle that supports their unique definition of Fabulously Successful. An American living in Paris, an international entrepreneur and a highly fulfilled mother to her three sons, Dawn is living her dream and wants to inspire you to do the same. She believes that if you are not living a life you love, perhaps it is time to make a change. To learn more about Dawn, Fabulously Successful and how you too can share your message with the world you are invited to go to: www.fabulouslysuccessful.com

CHAPTER **2**

Closet Guru - Coming Out of the Closet with My Own Unique Gift

Michelle Pozon

The name of my business, Closet Guru, is not just about clothing for me: it is a play on words, it means coming out into the open and loving from and living with my passions. It means no longer hiding from my greatness and accepting that it is only in doing what I love that I can excel and thrive.

I've been in love with creating outfits all my life. My parents saw it as a "charming hobby." I believed in their counsel, but I also knew the love and joy I felt when I made my mom feel beautiful.

Growing up in South East Asia in the 70s and 80s, my favorite moments were styling my mother's outfits for the occasional Embassy Ball. I can still picture a six-year-old me, standing behind my mom as she looked into the mirror, beaming at her own reflection. She was lovely already, but in those moments it was clear to me that I was giving her a special gift, and I felt so incredibly proud and thankful that I could do such a thing.

As I got older, my charming hobby evolved into an "impractical distraction." I was advised that my time would be better spent

7

studying "so that I could grow up to be a doctor or a lawyer (or at least marry one)."

I tried to make my parents proud and kept my fantasies to myself, but deep down I knew: "One day I will live in Paris, be married to an adoring French husband and have a gorgeous child. And, I will be helping women feel BEAUTIFUL."

Fast forward thirty-nine years and here I am in Paris. I am not sure if I pursued my dream, but I am sure my dream pursued me.

******

By the age of twenty-three, I had grown up into neither a doctor nor a lawyer; I was miserable working for Citibank in San Francisco. I never studied art or design, but I started my first clothing label, just to stop my then boyfriend from calling me a "chicken." Soon my collections were selling in trendy boutiques in the Marina and Pacific Heights areas; I was designing wedding dresses, and helping friends shop and vamp up their closets.

When my brother died in 1994 I moved to New York to be near my sister, and started my second label there. I was twenty-eight. Although my accounts included Saks Fifth Avenue, Henri Bendel, Harvey Nichols and Bergdorf Goodman, my "success" led me to tears. With the exception of a few moments of creative bliss, I found myself feeling abandoned, too much in my own head.

At tradeshows and when meeting my clients, the talk was always about numbers, terms of sale, and sell through dates. I did not hear that I was helping anyone, or that my dresses made women feel pretty. The bigger my business grew, the smaller I felt and I could not understand why I was struggling.

In 2001, my French-born, New York-raised husband - neither a doctor nor a lawyer - started talking about living in Paris. Wanting a fresh start we moved here in 2004. It was my childhood dream but that was not at all in the forefront of my mind.

Within a few months I got pregnant and we decided to stay. In 2005 our beautiful son was born and in 2006 I started a children's wear label. Hoping that I had finally found my way to a sense of fulfillment I teamed up with a business partner and was buoyed by the inspiration of my son.

Once again, four years into our business and just as we began to realize success, I started to crumble. With much grief, and for a song, I sold my share of the business. I cried and huddled into a corner, ashamed of myself for what I believed then to be "letting my son down", and giving away another one of my creations. My grief continued for months until I finally surrendered. I read books by Louise Hay and Marianne Williamson and I taught myself to meditate.

I spent two years in what I call "meditation hibernation," my sole goal to feel *every* emotion in kindness, without judgment. I prayed for answers and when no answers seemed to come I consoled myself by going into our closets, clearing out clutter, organizing and reorganizing my home until it "felt right." I chanted encouraging mantras to myself as I cleared out the excess: "I am beloved and worthy, just as I am" and a recent favorite, from Mastin Kipp: "Everything happens *for* me, not *to* me."

When my home was in tip-top shape I started bringing order to my friends' closets, shopping with them, helping them with their wardrobe concerns. Often one would nudge me jokingly, "are you sure you don't want me to pay you for this?" Then one day, as I was walking home, my childhood daydream came into consciousness. Lights and whistles went off in my head. I was *here* in Paris, with my loving, beautiful family and I was helping women feel beautiful!

I shrieked, ran home and called up some friends. "I got it," I pronounced into the phone, laughing and crying all at once, "Yes, I would LOVE to help women FEEL beautiful. I'm going to be the Closet Guru in Paris."

Doubts continued, but I kept meditating, asking the Universe only for my highest good; my prayers were answered with blessings every day. Word got out and Closet Guru was born – I had four clients in the first week!

Soon I was redoing four closets in a month, bringing joy to women's spaces. I replaced their clutter and confusion with confidence and grace.

Today, I am out of the closet, and have given myself permission to experience the joy of playing in closets again. My perspective has changed; I'm not trying to be anything other than myself, and I'm thankful for who I am.

I'm also thankful for my family. For most of my life they gave me financial freedom. I was never hungry. I always had a beautiful home. I could always go where I wanted to go and start a business without a loan. In exchange, I thought I had to be something that they understood, to make them proud.

I used to be embarrassed to lead a "charmed life". I felt so "lucky" not to have the challenges other people faced. I crippled myself with feelings of guilt. I tried to do what I thought I "should" do, instead of what I wanted to do.

Finding style in chaotic spaces may not be something everyone understands but my family has always supported me in their own way. I spent many years trying to prove to them that I could thrive despite what I saw as their lack of faith in me. I now see that it was my faith I needed more than theirs.

It has taken me forty years to recognize that it was me who neglected my childhood dream. My parents may have not understood my passions, but I was the one living in denial. They gave simply because they love me. I now see that real gratitude would be to use my gifts in service precisely because only I can.

They never asked me to prove myself. I gave myself that burden and it is something I have been unlearning, one second at a time, over the last two years.

******

My business is small but growing. I meditate daily, nurturing the inner child that I shushed all those years. I help women free themselves of excess and encourage them to get in touch with their dreams instead of neglecting them. Women trust me with their vulnerability, humbling me with that awesome responsibility.

I am not here to make a person over, but to mirror their beauty when they can't see it. I am here to encourage them to find themselves in the face of fashionable "must haves" and peer or societal pressures.

My services are playfully named: "the Closet Cleanse", "Shopping Expedition", "Soul Styling" and "Destination Chic". My clients and I are mutually engaged and enriched, in fun.

Ever since I started Closet Guru, I've caught myself singing "Beautiful Boy" by John Lennon. The verse below is one that my dad used to hum from time to time:

> *Before you cross the street*
> *Take my hand*
> *Life is what happens to you*
> *While you're busy making other plans ...*

In trying to be a success in the eyes of others, I was busy "making other plans", and yet, without my realizing, my dreams were unfolding. Despite the confusion and misery and self-doubt, those earlier years were essential. I honed my skills as a fashion designer and learned the tools of the trade, which I now use in service for my clients.

While the verse above is quoted often, the one below is the one I sing all the time:

> *Before you go to sleep*
> *Say a little prayer*
> *Every day in every way*
> *it's getting better and better... Beautiful, beautiful,*
> *beautiful....*

My dreams have found me and I now see how everything has happened and continues to happen in perfect time. As I bike home each day after work, I see my mother's smile. That glorious image is mirrored back at me every time I see my clients beam at their own reflection.

Photo by: Claire Morris

Michelle Pozon

Mother, Wife, Closet Guru, and Philanthropist. After 20 years as a fashion designer, with an international clientele, Michelle found her passion by focusing on the individual.

With Closet Guru, she empowers women to clear out the superfluous and uncover their true style and grace.

After the devastation of Typhoon Haiyan, in November 2013, she co-founded **Paris for the Philippines**, an international nonprofit group, dedicated to bringing aid and support to those affected by the tragedy. **PFTP** hosts live fundraisers and a curated website which highlights the best of Filipino and French worlds and promotes inter-cultural appreciation and exchange.

Contact Michelle at closetguruparis@gmail.com or through www.parisforthephilippines.com

CHAPTER 3

A Joyful Heart Makes a Cheerful Face

Mady Mendes

My name is Mady and I was born and grew up in the city of love: Paris. My parents come from Guinée Bissau, a small country in West Africa. They came to live in France for a better future. My mother never went to school so she can't read and can barely speak French and yet she is a very strong and confident woman. My father, who only went to school for a very short period of time, is joyful and funny.

I have so much admiration for my parents because they are proof that you can start from the bottom and reach the top. They left their village for a country where they didn't speak the language and didn't know the culture.

Their journey to find a better life could have turned into a nightmare but it ended up as the best dream ever. My parents have been a source of great inspiration for me my entire life. They taught me that a dream is worth pursuing and that even if the way is not always clear, you must believe in where your heart is directing you.

When I was younger I was very shy; I always seemed to be wearing a sad face. I was not at all confident and I felt so lonely. People would call me "the stupid girl". I was always asking myself, "Why do other people see me as stupid when I don't?" I couldn't find an answer to that question so I simply began to allow myself to think that maybe they were right, that I was stupid. As a result, my grades at school were not good.

When I reached my teen years, I loved to spend my time on the internet; Myspace and MSN were my favorites. I was so simple, quiet, and absolutely not girly. Somewhere along the way, I decided I wanted to be a flight attendant. It became my main goal. I knew that I couldn't be shy and be a flight attendant, though, so I promised myself to work as hard as I could to gain the necessary confidence in myself to go and make my dreams come true.

It was about this time that due to my motivation and determination, my results at school began to get better. In high school I chose a special customer service course that required an internship in retail, knowing that this would help me with my shyness and force me to talk to strangers. I successfully graduated and got my driving license at the same time. These two victories proved to me that I can be fearless about life.

By this time I was stronger and more confident and I was finally able to answer that question: "Why do other people see me as stupid when I don't?" The answer I found was: "I was listening to liars".

After my graduation I needed to learn to speak English. That was the last thing missing before I could reach my goal of becoming a flight attendant.

I decided to be a *"fille au pair"* and move to the UK where I could really learn the language. I realized I was about to live the same experience that my parents had gone through: going to a country where I didn't speak the language, didn't know the culture, and didn't know anyone. On top of that, I would be living with strangers whom I only knew through email.

It turned out that I was lucky: the family was perfect. The children were the brothers I never had, and the parents were some of the wisest people I had met.

For nearly two years in the UK I went to school with foreign students who wanted to learn English. I wanted to learn fast so I registered at the library and found a passion for reading; I was able to read a book in just two days.

Even though so much was happening, I still felt like "the simple girl". I knew that something was still missing so I decided to begin to take care of myself. I started with my hair: I found a hairdresser and did a "big chop" then every month I had my hair done. I changed my fashion style and learned to apply makeup by watching videos on YouTube. All of this brought out the best in me; I was an independent grown-up young woman.

I came back to France speaking perfect English. Somehow I knew that Paris was the place I would fulfill my dreams, just as my parents had fulfilled theirs here. Unfortunately for me, the economic crisis had hit and airlines were lowering their staff numbers. I decided to go back to what I had done in my very first job and became a sales assistant. I got a job in a fashion retail store and worked there for two years; but during this time, another passion was starting to grow in my heart: makeup. I was constantly watching videos of girls showing different makeup looks and using different beauty products. I was obsessed and started spending all of my money on makeup, trying new products, testing the latest trends. I had become a makeup addict.

One day I realized that spending all my money on makeup felt very selfish. With all of that money I could have brought so much joy to my family and people around me. I could have made great memories. I hated this part of me.

From that day, I promised myself I would help more. I decided to mix my passion with generosity and I came up with the idea to create a makeup line that would bring joy to others' lives. I named my brand Mazinha Cosmetics. Mazinha is the name of my mother – I wanted to use her name because she has always inspired me, she is the strongest woman I know.

My company's slogan is: "A joyful heart makes a cheerful face". It means that when you are happy inside, you are able to show your real beauty. My goal with Mazinha Cosmetics is to collaborate with charity associations to help raise money, materials or medicine that can change people's lives - there are so many problems in the world that it seems unfair to try to solve only one.

Also, for me, fashion and makeup are inseparable so I want to feature unknown talented fashion designers to give them the chance to show their work to the world. It is my wish that by wearing Mazinha cosmetics you will know that you are making someone's life better; you are a joy maker. My motivation is to develop greatness in others because it's a mission that will never end. I will give all I have for the rest of my life for Mazinha Cosmetics.

I need to inspire, to give, to share, to love and say I was here. I will help all those I see in need every single day that God opens my eyes because tomorrow doesn't exist, it is today that counts. As an old epitaph says: "What I gave, I have; what I spent, I had; what I kept, I lost".

Joel Osteen says, "Do all you can to make your dreams come true." You simply have to start with what you have, cultivate a positive mind and a winner's attitude, use humble words, put a smile on what you do and you can succeed at almost anything for which you have unlimited enthusiasm".

Never let anyone lie to you about who you are and what you can or can't do. I have learned that to be a strong person you have to make your own decisions. If people talk negatively about you, live and work so that no one will believe in them.

Every successful person is being helped by someone else, have a grateful heart and be quick to acknowledge those who help. Make yourself indispensable to somebody; a smile is a gift you can give every day. Zig Ziglar said, "You will always have everything you want in life if you will help enough other people get what they want".

Journalist Pauline Phillips said there are two types of people in the world: those who come into the room and say, "Here I am!" and those who come in and say, "Ah, there you are!" Which one are you?

"I will not let anyone walk through my mind with their dirty feet."
Gandhi

"Unless life is lived for others, it is not worthwhile". Mother Theresa

Photo by: Olivier Desaleux

Mady Mendes

Madeleine (Mady) Mendes, is an entrepreneur and founder of Mazinha cosmetics. Her parents immigrated from Guinée Bissau in west Africa to Paris, France where Mady was born and raised. After graduating, she resided for nearly two years in the United kindom where she found her love for makeup and then returned to Paris to begin her cosmetic business. Mady believes her main purpose in life is to be a philanthropist. www.mazinhacosmetics.com

CHAPTER 4

Paris is a Place to Dream...

Jennifer Manson

Paris, for me, is a place to dream. Walking by the river, or sitting in a café, looking across at light stone buildings, one balcony after another promising the possibility of a glamorous, light-filled life, I never fail to reconnect with that deep part of myself, the part that knows the wildest of my ambitions, the truest expression of my heart.

My first experience of Paris was at eighteen, the year I finished school, travelling with my cousin, Richard. It felt a long way from our home in New Zealand. We saw the seedy side of the city, staying in a railway hotel where – whether by neglect or design – the curtains on my window didn't quite meet. We went to the Eiffel Tower and I bought a beret and fell in love with Paris.

The next experience, not quite five years later, was on honeymoon at age twenty-two. I remember the glorious sensation of waking up, married, and looking out at the dawn light over the rooftops.

Since then I've been back many times. From our home in Hampshire, England, where we spent seven years while our children were young, it was my haven, my escape. I'd get on the train on a Saturday morning, allow my thoughts to roam and settle on the train, then wander in a dream through the beautiful streets for the endless thirty hours before I headed home again to my family.

My favourite district is the 6th arrondissement, the famous Left Bank, where philosophers Sartre and de Beauvoir drank coffee and discussed their view of life; where Hemingway strolled and Oscar Wilde died. The streets are clean here, washed by patient men with their street sweeping machines and more frequently by the spectacular Paris rain, coming fast and brief, as it so often does, just enough time to wish for an umbrella before it is over.

I have my favourite places, my favourite pieces of art: Eugène Delaplanche's statues of Eve in the Musee d'Orsay; the Cour Marly in the Louvre with its cathedral-like whispering echoes and silvery light. When I meet friends I always take them on the same tour, of those same places, never tiring; and now, an addition, the statue of my role model, Joan of Arc, on the corner of rue de Rivoli and rue des Pyramides, opposite the Tuileries garden.

We've moved around a lot: Cambridge, England, where we married, back to New Zealand to have our children; back to England, to Hampshire, then New Zealand again, and now France, in the wilds of the Breton countryside.

Looking back, my life has been a series of leaps. Each time we've moved countries there has been the element of the unknown. My biggest leap was as a writer, sending my books out, braving the opinions of others, trusting that speaking from my heart was more important than staying safe; trusting that speaking my truth was the greatest gift I could give to the world.

Then, as a writer, it was a leap to leave my home, where I sold books wherever I went, to live in a non English-speaking country; but ever since my first trip to Paris it has been a dream to live in France and write here. When the chance came my choice was clear: I took a deep breath, took that next leap...

French countryside is like a different country from cosmopolitan Paris. Like any country, the rural atmosphere and pace of life are quieter and slower than in the capital; and Brittany, in particular, has a mystical quality, with its standing stones, its ancient legends.

So what about me, my writing career, after that leap? That was a challenge. At the time I arrived here, in 2011, I had six novels published. I was working on another, but somehow it wasn't flowing like they did back home. My gut told me it was time to stop, do things differently. But what? Do what?

I consulted my intuition. The answer came, unmistakable: "There's nothing to do. Do nothing." What?!?

Maybe I needed that. Maybe I needed to learn to slow down, or even stop; to look around me and experience life, right now. As long as I could remember I'd been running at life pretty hard: my university degree, career, building a business, and alongside it all, writing. Always writing. Now it was time to stop.

I protested against it. I dabbled here and there in lots of things – I couldn't just do nothing, after all. Could I?

Eventually the message became so loud I couldn't ignore it any longer. Do nothing! Stop! So eventually, I did. "Okay," I said, "All right. I get it. I'll do nothing." And finally, I learned how to accept it, and rest.

It was as if I had flicked a switch, as if life had just been waiting for me to get that lesson, appreciate where I was and what I had before sending me off on the next adventure. It was only days later that I met Lucy Whittington, a genius at identifying genius, who coached me into my new career, writing books with experts, and brought me my first exciting wave of clients.

I work with my clients to bring out their voice, their genius, to get their message out into the world in book form. It's such a privilege to learn from them, to draw them out, to show them their uniqueness, and help them reveal that uniqueness to the world.

I feel so fortunate to live in the age I live in. My first novel was published two weeks after the first Kindles arrived in New Zealand, allowing me to distribute internationally from the first moment of publication. The rise of print-on-demand publishing means that I, and my clients, can start slow and easy, sell our books through any of the world's book websites, buy a few copies to carry around with us for the people we meet face to face and allow those sales to organically grow.

It is no longer the big dragon to slay that it used to be, writing and publishing books. It's easy – practically – although the demons of fear of rejection still rise up; but I'm a master at conquering those, and helping my clients conquer them, too.

The miracles of the Internet, Skype and email are a Godsend, making doing business internationally the simplest of things. I have clients in Wales, England and New Zealand, and occasionally calls with Australia and the US scheduled into my day, as well.

For me, gregarious and voluble as I am, living physically isolated has been a huge challenge. Far from my many friends in the various countries I have lived, and with my French still far less fluent than my English, it has stretched me in ways I didn't anticipate; and in the process, shown me more of myself.

Sometimes the absence of something teaches us more about it than when we have it in our lives day to day. I took conversation for granted, didn't realize how much it fed me and was necessary for my happiness and peace. Now, when I see a friend face to face, or travel to England and have a cheerful chat with the person on the checkout at the supermarket, I know the huge blessing that is. I feel their physical presence in my heart and soul, and I am grateful for it.

I feel energy more consciously now. I notice much more how the energy in a room shifts when people walk in or out of it; I notice how a change of mood in someone I'm with causes a shift in my own state; I'm learning how I can bring people up with my optimism, how encouraging them changes the way they feel – I feel that so strongly now, because of these years I've spent away from it day-to-day.

Now, in my next phase, my next leap, I've begun making journeys, guided by intuition, all over the world, to see the people in my life whom I love. I tell them the things I want to tell them, say the things intuition guides me to say. I tell them the difference they make in the world. One of my joys is to point out their strengths, their talents, the way they contribute to the people around them, and to see how that operates as a life-giving force, like water on a parched plant. They hear my appreciation, my love, and they blossom.

This, above anything, is what France has taught me – how to translate my love and joy in others into something that deeply touches them, that makes their lives, and the lives of those around them, the people they touch, better, too.

Photo by: Paul Manson

Jennifer Manson

Jennifer Manson is The Flow Writer, helping clients who have an important message to share to bring that message to the page. Jennifer is the author of six novels and one non-fiction title Easy – Stories from an effortlessly created life about how we can make the practical aspects of life easy, so we can get the important things done. www.theflowwriter.com.

CHAPTER 5

Paris, Je t'aime
Julia Willard

Sometimes in order to be our best selves, we need to remove ourselves from our current situations and get not only to a mental space that offers something new, but also to a physical location that provides us an elevated sense of being. I have considered at times that everyone has that place – a place in the world that maybe takes years to find, but a place where one feels best with oneself; where being in the flow just happens effortlessly, where a person feels nurtured to be the inspired co-creator of her life that she's meant to be.

I have discovered that I experience an elevated sense of myself when I am in France. It started with my first taste of the language and was solidified when I was sixteen years old and visited Paris for the first time. Every time I return I am transformed. I don't know why, I don't know how. I don't know why for me this transformative place has to be one of the most expensive cities in the world, but I do know that it's not surprising that I would feel that transformation in a place widely regarded as the most beautiful city in the world.

I was never dubbed a particularly outgoing girl as a kid. People would look at me and deem me, rather, as timid and reserved. To this day, I have friends who have known me since childhood and are astounded at how I turned out. I like to think of myself as a work in progress, but I understand their reactions. How *did* sweet little ever-obedient Julie end up cavorting about Paris?

My love for France started before I ever stepped foot in it. French was the first language I learned beyond my native English, uttering my first French words (with one hell of a bad accent, no doubt) "Je m'appelle Julie" in Kindergarten French class. We learned very little those first couple of years. Could my memory be accurate that I really felt disappointment in my teacher that we were learning this language at such a slow pace? I had had my first taste of French, and I was craving far more beyond the days of the week and the colors.

From grade school on I was a devoted Francophile, always looking for more assignments and more ways to pick up the language quickly. In high school, having missed the chance the previous summer to travel to France with my French teacher for five weeks, I was determined to secure my spot early when she announced another trip to Paris and Provence over an extended Spring Break.

Despite not being able to see the Eiffel Tower from the airport as I had expected, Paris met or exceeded all my glowing expectations. I fell for the architecture, the attention to detail, the beauty, the parks and gardens, the bread, the sweets, and even more so for the melodic language that had first enraptured me eleven years earlier. I no longer had a crush on France, I was in love.

Next, I set my sights on studying abroad in Paris during university. While my high school classmates asked thoughtful questions on campus visits about job placement and rankings, I was interested in little more than how the study abroad program was and was there one in France.

In the end, because I was pursuing a double major in French and International Business, I had no choice but to go to the French city that had the Business program: Dijon. Being in Dijon widened my interest in and deepened my love for France, and ultimately myself. I still hadn't pinpointed why I felt such a draw to this country (the origin of *je ne sais quoi* perhaps?) but I was subconsciously receiving the message loud and clear that it was where I felt best.

Although at that point I had only spent five days in the Capital, I still felt drawn to Paris; I didn't know then that it would secure a very special place in my heart and memory as I was finishing up my semester abroad. Perhaps that is when I realized just how fabulously full of surprises Paris can be.

Then came "the real world". You know, that place where you're taught to do something socially-deemed "sensible" with yourself? Well, "sensible" has never really been part of my vocabulary. I was always eager for adventure beyond a desk and a cubicle, preferably surrounded by the song of a Romance language and the aromas of freshly baked breads and *pâtisseries*.

I was simultaneously getting clearer on what I wanted for my life. I knew I desired a life rich in culture, beauty, nature time and challenges. My personal spiritual journey led me to notice that beauty is truly all around us. I also noticed that when we are feeling good in life, we are on a path of positive further creation. Sure, we are naturally drawn to certain things that we enjoy doing or being a part of; that is logical. However, we do not always give ourselves permission to receive exactly that which we desire.

That feeling of a magnetic draw to something is foreign to no one. We have an inner knowing that is truly spiritual *à la base*, and yet we don't always give ourselves permission to submit to that draw. Our heads get in the way and we talk ourselves out of those big dreams, the ones like moving to Paris for the simple reason that it's where we feel best in the world. I decided – at least on this one topic – that I was going to give myself what I knew makes me feel good. I had to move to Paris.

Paris has been instrumental in the development of my personal creative endeavors, albeit mostly subconsciously. It gets in your eyes, in your expectations; it even creeps into your hope for the world. That attention to detail that manifests in the French traditions of *le luxe*, hospitality, and creativity in general is still prevalent in everyday life here. It's no coincidence that tens of millions of people come every year to experience magnificent manmade beauty. It's a place where people feel more alive just by virtue of having seen others create in their own unique ways.

Almost exactly two years ago, a friend sat across the table from me and asked me why I wasn't creating in *my* unique way, that is, sharing all this beauty through my photography. You see, I have been photographing what seems like every moment of my European adventure since film was still the norm.

Over the years, to share my life and adventures with friends and family back home, I created online photo albums of my life in Paris, and eventually Amsterdam too. The feedback I got was so positive that this friend thought I was crazy not to be printing and making products out of my photographs. It took me a few months, but eventually I jumped into a new venture that married my loves of photography, beauty and Europe. I continue to share my stories and my adventures of life abroad through my photography company Falling Off Bicycles, which keeps me connected with the cities I love and those who share that love.

Somewhere along the way I understood that what I was doing was deliberately creating my life; that Paris and my comings and goings were every bit my choice stemming from intentions - both conscious and unconscious - that I had set forth some time ago. I hadn't always seen them coming into fruition, but when they arrived I remembered that letting go and – as clichéd as it sounds – going with the flow had been of paramount importance to them manifesting. Paris is the place that has provided the daily challenge, the daily beauty, and even the daily nature time that I crave. It may not always be the place that provides that elevated sense of being for me, and it certainly isn't that for everyone, but there is an undeniable magic that resides in this city that so many people find themselves seduced by.

At some point in the last few years, I made note of a quote by Howard Thurman that struck me as the answer to the ultimate question: "Don't ask what the world needs. Ask what makes you come alive, and go do it. Because what the world needs is people who have come alive."

For me, Paris has been that place the last few years and I am incredibly grateful I have been able to make it happen. It got me into my flow and into that space of feeling my elevated sense of self. Whether your transformative space is a physical or spiritual place, find it, cherish it and reside there as often as possible.

** NOTE: The author uses French terms from time to time, which are likely self-evident in English translation, but are more perfectly expressed through the French term or word.

Photo: Author's personal collection

Julia Willard

Self-proclaimed *intrepid voyageuse* Julia Willard has made a life out of always looking for new places to live, explore, photograph, and write about. Never without a camera in her bag and a notebook at hand, she captures the beauty around her to share in hopes of inspiring others to pursue their respective passions. www.fallingoffbicycles.com

CHAPTER 6

My Sight Seeking Delight
Karen Reb Rudel

My name is Karen Reb Rudel and I own a walking tour company in Paris, Sight Seeker's Delight. Instead of doing what I normally do in my work and tell the history of Paris, I'm going to do a rare thing and share the history of myself in Paris!

Years ago, I had a 'past life reading' and the fortune teller explained to me that I had lived in Paris in five past lives. She said that if you feel comfortable somewhere, maybe you've been there before and I really think there's truth in that.

Paris always felt like home, from the very beginning, even though I had really no interest in it when I came to Europe other than for a croissant and to see the Eiffel Tower!

Until I arrived, that is.

Paris is one of those unique places that if you give it half a chance, it will snatch you up and never let you leave. There's something magical in seeing the monuments and beauty every day and yes, there are the French people but everything else that France has to offer as well (I'm married to a Frenchman so ladies and gentlemen I've earned the right to joke about them!)

Let me backtrack to the beginning, which seems like a good place to start my story. One of my best friends and I decided to do a ten-day trip to Europe. Well, ten days turned into one month. Then our thinking went, "If we're going to schlep all the way over, well, we'd better make it two months". Now, I've been here fifteen years.

It really happened in the blink of an eye. My friend and I were traveling around and staying in youth hostels, I kept pulling out my flute since I thought I might find a good band to jam with, Europe-style. We had traveled to London, Amsterdam and Paris and finally one day I found a musician in Paris, Simi Ol of ARRR Force.... and Voilà, as they say!

In between music projects I was driving around France, seeing it all… but then serendipity struck: our car broke down and I was forced to move back to Paris. Imagine being forced to move to Paris! I was 'grounded' for a while, so I started to teach English and babysit (like many expats do here).

My parents came to visit after I'd been in Paris for a while, so I took them around to see the city. I knew nothing about French history at the time but I pointed out the Sacré-Cœur and my mom exclaimed, "You'd make a fabulous tour guide!" You know, everybody should always listen to their mother…

By that time I was working at a youth hostel and I started to learn and research fun facts of Paris, and then take people out to see the things I was talking about. Before I knew it, I was giving tours on a regular basis. After that, I met my French husband and that really cinched the deal about me staying in Paris!

At the same time, I took my mother's advice and opened up Sight Seeker's Delight to give tours on my own. Since I got pregnant a few months later, however, not much happened for a while (other than my belly growing bigger every day but that, my friends, is a whole other book). Now we have the cutest French-American boy and it's amazing to watch his little brain soak up two languages, and then somehow explain himself and be able to communicate in both.

I hadn't yet made a name for myself in the tourism world, so I didn't have many tours to give at the very start. But it grew, and fast! A friend put my barely-there company on a little site called TripAdvisor, which I wasn't even familiar with at the time. I remember the first couple of reviews came in and all of a sudden I was number twenty-five and boy, was I thrilled! Within three months of my baby's life, out of nowhere, I was in the Top Ten and have held that position for the past three years.

Things have changed enormously in the travel industry. Twenty years ago, if you didn't have a *Let's Go* or a *Lonely Planet* guide, you were pretty lost on your travels. You were just moving around and hoping to find a hostel or a hotel that was safe. I've been front and center witnessing the change the Internet has made in traveling – the world has exploded for travelers! Fear of the unknown is put on the back burner because you can research anything and see what other travelers think of it. But since it's an 'everyone knows everything' kind of industry, to be a success you have to set yourself apart and I knew that from the beginning.

Figuring out what I wanted to give travelers who toured with me was easy – my goal is "edutainment": education with entertainment. Everyone who finds Sight Seeker's Delight wants to go on vacation and have a laugh. It's no secret that lots of people in Anglophone countries have a little bit of Attention Deficit Disorder... They don't always want to be bogged down with details they can't compute, especially when there's so much else to do besides just hearing a slew of names and dates. Paris is a completely different culture and there's a huge desire for travelers to see the people, learn about the culture and etiquette, see monuments, hear about the quirks and oddities that make France and the French so unique... they want to understand in a real-life and practical way what the French have given us, and what they've contributed to the world. People come to Paris for so much more than just the Eiffel Tower.

All those things are exactly what I want to share with the world, so I formed Sight Seeker's Delight based on that idea and I think a key to my success was sticking with it. I decided that I wanted all the guides to be entertainers: actors, musicians, comedians, or simply people who have the enthusiasm to really share their love of the city with travelers, whether they are on their first visit to Paris or their hundredth!

I've read over 100 books (and counting) on Paris in order to write my tours; I'm not a historian but this is sort of my own personal PhD program. There's this idea that if you don't have a PhD in this or that, you're not an expert... but let's not forget that Albert Einstein taught himself calculus! I consider myself a self-taught expert, though of course there's always more to learn.

What I'm doing is saving travelers a lot of time because I'm taking out all the bad pages that aren't essential or interesting — and there are plenty, believe me, in a country with such a long history. I love to give travelers super-memorable anecdotes, and later at cocktail parties they'll have these amazing bits of trivia to tell, people will flock to them and champagne will be poured left and right! That's my dream for everyone, to come away from the tour with a slew of unique stories that they can actually remember and share with their friends.

I honestly think I have the greatest job in the universe. I love meeting people from all over the world. Some of them have visited Paris over and over again, and I get a kick out of still being able to find them a nook or cranny somewhere that they hadn't seen, or tell them a story they'd never heard.

I take very small groups out touring and one thing I say is, "This group of people might never be assembled ever again, so if you from Jersey have something to say to you from Glasgow, today's the day." That's another thing that is so satisfying for me in my work – I'm not only sharing Paris, but also bringing people together. It's not uncommon for me to find connections between travelers and myself, even! The world is not as big as we have the tendency to think.

I'm overwhelmingly happy that I have this successful business in Paris and that it's a pleasure to go to work every day. For me, success is waking up each morning and being happy with what you do, being excited to start the day. I know I'm very lucky to have that – though it was more than just luck, it's been hard work too! It's important to not be scared of putting yourself out there and going for your dream. Don't be shy, I always say. Not being shy was never, obviously, a problem for me – if you've met me even once you know this! – but it is simply the best advice for travelers, expats, and just everyone in general. You never know what's going to be right around the corner, who you'll meet or what you'll do and how that will change the course of your life. You've got to be willing to turn that corner though, and find out!

Photo by: Claire Thomas

Karen Reb Rudel

Born and raised in Johnstown, Pennsylvania, Karen grew up with the aspiration to be a comedian, a musician, or both. She went on to study drama at Temple University in Philadelphia and played in a series of bands. From the age of 30 until she got married, Karen was back and forth between Paris and Philadelphia, working on musical projects and touring. One day her parents came to visit Karen, and while she was showing them around, her mother exclaimed, "Karen, you would make a great tour guide!" That was the light bulb moment, and voila Sight Seeker's Delight unique walking tours was born. www.sightseekersdelight.com

═══════════════ Chapter 7

Nothing Ventured, Nothing Gained
Lesley Kirk Renaud

During my early years, I had a deep need to break away from the rural English countryside where everyday life runs like clockwork – beautiful setting, but same old cups of tea at breakfast, elevenses and of course "high tea" at four o'clock! I never quite got into this and wherever possible always endeavored to make each day a little more eventful.

Inside I had a need to move forward, a need to expand any topic of conversation that meant I was learning something new, a need to meet people who had more to say than the local gossip. Anything different - help! Life's for living and having fun, after all.

Perhaps traveling from a young age increased my need to discover new things. It was always evident to my family that one day I would be living somewhere other than Cheshire. When and how was totally unknown but it was clear that I would be doing something different than those around me then.

One fine day, fate played its hand - a Frenchman in my local pub! Unbelievable! He was so full of fun - so much for our preconceived ideas of the French. Little did I know I was going to fall in love! That definitely kept things interesting for the following days, months and eventually years.

My first trip to Paris – an invitation to attend a Lions club auction at the Hotel InterContinental – sent me into a small frenzy: "What to wear?" "How will I converse in French with the guests?" etc… I didn't speak a word of French!

It was so exciting jetting to the most famous city of all. I was on a high, with the adventure of going into the unknown, of meeting my future family and all the uncertainties that go with that.

The first view of La Tour Eiffel rising above majestically on the river bank was breathtaking. I remember saying that I would never tire of this view. The River Seine, Trocadero, the amazing unaffordable clothes shops, the French swaggering leisurely through the streets… That was a strange thing: no flamboyance, everything calm with sedate colors, not to mention that the ladies all wore flat shoes. I certainly looked like a foreigner in the city of lights.

I was ready for anything and everything, soaking up the differences. Even the air seemed different and I started to feel free, more alive. I could be anyone I wanted here in Paris!

The decision on my destiny was made and the following week I circulated my CV to international employment agencies and it and it happened! I got a job straight away in a large American company as a bi-lingual executive assistant. I returned to my then current job – heading up the recruitment side of an advertising agency – and with a few regrets I handed in my notice. My career had started off extremely well, but there was so much more to do in Paris!

One month later I was moving into a new flat – in Paris! Well nearly Paris – only fifteen minutes away and five minutes walk from my new job. No French required, thank goodness, it was my English which was precious to them – incredible!

That was the start of three years of enjoying the city lights, the good food and wine and my future husband, so terribly romantic and funny, always wanting to whisk me away somewhere new.

My first year was like being on holiday. I met Irish, French, Dutch, German, Americans, all lunching together for a whole two hours with wine – unheard of in England but normal practice in Paris. As friendships were made, dinner invitations began flowing. Gosh, now I had to start understanding French culinary skills. Eek! Not my forte at all. I regretted not staying home with my parents when I was younger to watch and learn how to cook, instead of speeding around with friends on bikes! How was I going to succeed at this?

I had little furniture and what I did have was certainly not the style I wanted for entertaining. The grand ideas of entertaining and protocol and etiquette I had been brought up with were putting me under pressure in this new part of my life.

Thank goodness, I discovered 'traiteurs' – it was completely acceptable in Paris to buy freshly made, ready-to-eat appetizers and goodies on the way home from work. The long hours of transport and work made this a great discovery, saving me so much time and effort after many a hard day's work. I was always ready to celebrate something/anything with my international friends and new French family!

After three years, my French was flowing and I moved to another international company, to a position with larger responsibilities. There was no stopping me. Life naturally got easier: the butchers, the bakers, the hairdressers, the supermarket – I was now *really* living the French life. My family and friends were very proud and I realized how much I had learned in such a short time.

At the same time, my job had become easy and I was not feeling stretched; for me this meant the starry-eyed and ambitious young woman arriving from Cheshire was now growing into someone different! Why did it no longer excite me?

I realized it was my constant ambition to be doing something different, learning, moving on and up. It is a really important part of me. I needed to move positions again, but to what? In France, you are quickly categorized so here I was, stuck in this role of bilingual Executive Assistant. Oouuuccchhh! Somehow, I created the opportunity to grow by landing the position of Customer Relations Manager. Now I would get to travel across Europe! This was great!

Then came the joy of my first son, which slightly changed the course of events. On my return to the company, they had relocated outside of the city so time to move on, yet again.

I was offered a fantastic position in advertising with the largest publishing company in the US, launching a luxury magazine across Europe where, this time, my French was an advantage! This meant relocating to England, a bigger house, and being close to my sisters, both of whom also had their first children by this time.

Although the job was fantastic, the most surprising thing happened: I realized I did not fit back easily into my old life, slow-paced with its typical routines. No dinner invitations during the week, no last minute parties – Paris was definitely calling me back!

It took just over a year to get the boxes packed back up and return to Paris, to our newly created duplex with fireplaces and ornate ceilings. Wow, things had moved on again.

My second son arrived and thanks to the good support systems in France, I was able to continue working in a high-level position as a fast paced Executive Assistant traveling across Europe organizing events for the company President and his executive team.

My responsibilities included organizing very large prestigious events – what a dream! I negotiated deals with top establishments, created international events, booked boats, helicopters and private jets. I was living in the fast lane, putting in many long hours, sometimes even working weekends – but I loved it and I was good at it!

My knowledge and experience with business strategy and goals in addition to the savoir-faire I had developed were rewarded with more responsibilities and I was offered the extra role of Culture Ambassador for Europe. Once again, however, my skills outweighed my job description and I began to feel stuck in the wheels of the organization.

It was time to take hold of my destiny; time to grow again; time to learn; time to realize that I can make things change the way I want them to. I can shape my own future.

What do I like doing best? What am I good at? What makes me tick?

They all seem simple questions but when you have to stake your future and income on doing what you love, you also need to be sure you are realistic about the risks and how you can mitigate them. Nothing ventured, nothing gained, however, especially when considering the fright of afternoon tea again!

I reflected on all the events I had organized professionally and personally, including my own wedding with international guests, family birthdays and romantic surprises.

It took a croissant and coffee – and a huge drink of courage – to create LKR International Events!

October 2012: LKR was officially registered. I booked an impressive stand at one of the largest Parisian wedding shows which actually created a buzz amongst the professionals too – this was exciting! Almost immediately I had a fantastic French couple wanting to marry in Crete. I confirmed the wedding ceremony with group travel, a private luxury villa, hotel accommodations and even negotiated with Greek suppliers, despite the complex administration.

That wedding was amazing and my business began to grow; my next special event was a surprise engagement at the Hôtel de Crillon for a very special Norwegian couple – absolutely rewarding! Since then business continues to grow at an impressive rate. French and international clients have booked weddings, anniversaries, engagement parties, teambuilding events and even birthday parties at private chateaux.

So here I am organizing, meeting inspiring people, helping clients to have their "made to measure" events, couples their bespoke "wedding of their dreams", creating unique moments – I am living my dream putting ideas and clients' visions into reality. My lifetime ambitions unfold hereon!

Photo by: Claire Morris

Lesley Kirk Renaud

British born Lesley Kirk-Renaud is founder of LKR International Events. Now based in Saint Germain-en-Laye just outside Paris, Lesley took her many years of corporate marketing and event planning experience to create her own high-end events company. LKR International specializes in creating and producing high quality events in France and across Europe from luxury weddings, to special birthdays to a romantic dinner in Paris to a festive baby shower as well as numerous options for organizing outstanding International corporate events. For tailor made service you are invited to contact: lkr@lkr-ie.com / www.lkr-ie.com

——————————————— CHAPTER **8**

A Year Ago Today
Addis Kassegn

A year ago today, I was living in San Diego California, I owned my house, I had a little dog, a partner and led my life as a marketing executive. Today, I live in Paris.

I categorize life into one of two lanes, tough lanes and cruising lanes. Everyone has had to make tough decisions in life; the degree of difficulty might vary depending on where we are at in life and whether or not we are equipped to face that decision. It was a tough lane that brought me to Paris.

"Oh dear, why would you quit such a great job and move to Paris?" said Janice, my new American friend. Americans are so friendly. Janice and I had just met on the flight from LA to CDG. Janice and her husband were heading to Paris to see the Tour Eiffel. I had just confided to them that I had purchased a one way ticket to Paris.

The look of utter shock on their faces made me nervous. I could feel the fear take over my body.

"But, Sweety, do you have a job waiting for you in Paris?" Janice asked, with the look of a concerned mother.

"No," I shook my head.

I excused myself and went to the bathroom. My body felt so heavy. Fear does that to me: in fear mode I feel alive… I also feel every part of my body movement get heavy and awkward. I washed my face; I could feel my stomach turning. I felt nausea take over, fear was all over me. I wanted the plane to stop. What was I thinking? How come no one stopped me from doing this? Janice was right; perhaps if my parents were in my life, they would have given me some sound advice.

******

My name is Addis, it means "new" in Amharic (the Ethiopian language). My parents are from Gonder, a northern town of Ethiopia. My father was an attorney by trade, then got into politics and became the Minister of Foreign Affairs. He married my mother and by the time their fifth child came along they wanted a new life, so they named me Addis and moved the whole family to Turkey. My father had taken an Ambassador job in Turkey, this would be a low key position that would allow him to focus on his family. My mother was a beautiful house wife.

In 1976, a black Christian family with five kids was not something that Turkish people were used to seeing. We were a show. My eldest brother, Mike, would always demand that we disperse in groups of two and that we keep our distance from each other.

Due to my parents' travels and lifestyle, we grew up learning five languages and we also developed a high sensitivity to different cultures and customs.

We lived in Turkey for seven years, then moved to Egypt, where my father continued his work as an Ambassador. We were in Egypt for twelve years. In 1996, Eritrea and Ethiopia were in a civil war and when my parents returned to Ethiopia, for my safety, they left me in Egypt in the care of catholic nuns. I was 16 years old at the time.

At first, I thought my parents would come back for me in a few months, but they didn't. Up to this point in my life I had not faced difficult decisions. Up to this point, I had only been in the cruising lane of life.

After finishing high school, I could no longer stay with the nuns so they helped me apply for college. The first tough decision I had to make was to leave the nuns, where I had lived for two years, and move to the US for college. I remember feeling so scared and not wanting to leave Pilinchi, the nun who had essentialy been my family for two years. Pilinchi hugged me longer than usual and whispered in my ear "you got this". Fear seeped into me, I was now truly on my own. At nineteen, I was heading to San Diego California, no parents and no nuns.

My first experience with culture shock was in the States: I was nineteen and passing through immigration. The agent asked me if I was an alien and I said no, I was Ethiopian, and then clarified by saying "in Africa" because he didn't seem to understand me.

Though the dream of Paris was what I had grown up with, I decided to go to college in the US for the simple reason that I had an uncle who lived there. The States seemed to suit me, so Paris stayed on hold while I built a life for myself.

In the first eight years that I lived in the US, I focused on building my life. I studied international business, did my MBA in Marketing, learned Spanish and became a marketing executive in a company that I loved.

And then life unraveled...

I recently learned a word in French "Bouscule" which means to be pushed.

It all happened very quickly. I left my house. I didn't want anything from this past life... Well, I took my cute outfits and my beautiful shoes. I just wanted a new start, in Paris no one would know my past. No one would ask me what happened. Or if I was okay. Or whisper around me.

"Did you see the photo he posted on Facebook? Can you believe he is with her?" I wanted to respond "Yes, I know, the man I loved for 15 years, is now with his assistant" ...

I am not sure why I assumed this stuff only happened to other people. Secretly, I thought only stupid women got cheated on. How could a smart woman not see this coming? Well, I answered my own question... I did not see this coming.

He wanted time to figure things out, so I left to follow my dream, the dream I had before tough lanes appeared in my life. I said goodbye to my friends and to my life in San Diego. I left behind my American dream, for a new life in Paris.

Paris Je T'aime? "Non, Merci"

My first week in Paris was tough, to say the least...

A lady stole my hat while I was shopping; a homeless man spat at me; an elderly lady asked me why I was smiling at her in the metro; no one would respond to me when I said hello; the clerks in the store all snubbed me. I thought I made a new friend at an expatriate meeting, but when I asked my potential friend if she would like to grab a coffee and chat she said, "Non, Merci". The weather was cold and the people colder. This was not the Paris I had imagined or visited many times. I wanted to go home.

I called my sister, I called my girlfriends and I could not tell them the truth. They all seemed to think that I was eating croissants and having espressos all day. Somehow complaining about Paris was not allowed. So, I didn't.

Then, I walked Paris everyday and fell in love with every part of it. I took a year to really rethink my whole being, to re-examine everything that I had taken for granted. After a year of reflection and meditation, it was clear: I wanted and needed to live in Paris, to go for a dream instead of using my past as an excuse for not going for it.

I've now been in Paris a year. I look back at my fears and I am so grateful that I felt the fear and yet forced on. Being here has taught me so many lessons about life and about myself.

Recently, a homeless man spat at me and I did something so unlike me... I spat back at him, we exchanged a neutral look and parted ways... I laughed alone just thinking of what possessed me to do this.

I am not a tough girl, but I feel stronger now. My feelings are not as easily hurt as they used to be, I am not as scared as I used to be about the unknown.

When faced with tough decisions, we can let fear freeze us or prevent us from doing what we want or we can feel the fear and force ahead.

When I decided to move to Paris I had so many fears. What would become of my career? Would I make new friends? What about my love life? What about the exchange rate? Do I have enough saved?

Now I can tell you all my worries were real, but things do find a way to work themselves out. I did meet new friends and I found a consulting job. Every day I walk through the streets of Paris. Having my lunch in front of Notre Dame is my reward for feeling the fear and going forward.

The toughest part of my move was making the decision. Once I made the decision, I spent all my energy on my action items instead of giving in to the fear. I quit my job, sold my car, rented a room in a house to save money. Everything I did was focused towards my Paris dream.

As I meet women, I see so many of us refraining from going after our dreams. I used to think that there was just 0 to 10 on the scale of happiness. In Paris, I have discovered a whole new scale of measuring happiness.

The lesson learned... face the fear and do it anyways.

Photo by: Claire Morris

Addis Kassegn

Addis Kassegn currently lives in Paris and works with business owners in Europe and the US to help them develop their business strategy and market their products and services. Addis has lived in Paris, Spain, the USA, Egypt and Turkey. She is fluent in English, French, Arabic and Spanish. Addis has a bachelor's degree in international business and an MBA in marketing. With 16 years of experience in business development and marketing, Addis helps most of her clients by analyzing their business and applying the appropriate marketing initiatives.

======================= CHAPTER 9

My Soul Mate

Alecia Caine

If a place can be a soul mate then mine is France. This love affair with France and all things French began when I was a young child in elementary school and one of the moms volunteered to teach us some French phrases and songs. As simple as it was just listening to *Frères Jacques* and *Sur le Pont D'Avignon* and counting *un, deux, trois, quatre, cinq...* it was music to my ears and I fell in love with the romantic sound of the French language.

After that first encounter, I began my life-long quest for knowledge of French culture and discovered a country rich with the best life has to offer. As a university student, I minored in French as I studied international economics, and devoured French literature, French art, French cookbooks and French *Vogue*. I was mesmerized by Voltaire, Baudelaire, Victor Hugo, Camus, Maupassant, St. Exupery and Sartre and even starred as the foppish Monsieur Jourdain in our drama class production of Moliere's *Bourgeois Gentihomme*.

Every region in France has something unique to offer: Parisian sophistication and style, fashion and food, chocolate and cheese, perfumes and pastries, scandalous history and old farmhouses, not to mention the wines. France has it all. I've been coming back to France for over 30 years, and when I'm not in France, I long to be there.

My first trip was with my father and sister when I was eighteen. My wonderful dad recognized my passion and as a high school graduation gift he gave me a six-week voyage, driving the small country lanes in a tiny stick shift Renault. From the *haute couture* houses of Paris to the beaches of Normandy, we saw the towns and sights that inspired Monet, tasting camembert cheese and cider along the way.

We skirted around the rugged coastline of Brittany, visiting the mystical Mont St. Michel and St. Malo while eating crepes and salty caramel. In the Loire Valley I imagined myself as a princess in a chateau and in Burgundy we drove through sunflower fields as far as the eye could see. I loved the Dordogne for its natural beauty, rock formations, truffles and foie gras and Provence for its fragrant lavender fields and charming old farmhouses with blue shutters. From St. Tropez to Nice I was dazzled by the glitz and ritz of the Cote d'Azur and ate the most amazing food and wine in Alsace.

I wanted to stay... but I didn't. Instead I returned home, got married, had children, eventually got divorced and became a CPA. The highlight of these years was raising my sons to be sweet, wonderful, successful, happy men. But it was tough as a single mom and I had to put my dreams to live in France on hold. I learned how to "make it" professionally and financially but working sixty hour weeks in a CPA firm was like trying to stuff a square peg in a round hole. The environment was inhospitable for this creative lover of French culture and mom to two boys.

When my children were in elementary school, I mustered the courage to leave my safe job and pursue freelance accounting which was more compatible with the lifestyle I desired. With more control over my time, I soon discovered another passion: inspiring women to be successful in their own business and live their dreams, which led me to consulting women business owners on entrepreneurship.

I was very happy working part-time, picking my children up from school and taking them to the beach while earning as much income as

I had before when I was exhausted all the time. But part of me was still missing, my feminine self, the part that was nurtured when I was in France. At the age of forty-four I reached a major turning point in my life. My sons were growing up and I would soon be left with an empty nest. What was next for me? I finally had more freedom to pursue my dreams, but what were my dreams? I had lost touch with them.

After a lot of soul searching, journal writing, vision boarding and coaching, connecting to my femininity and spirituality, I remembered my passion for France! A few action steps got me closer to my goal to live part-time in France and part-time in California, which at the time seemed an impossible dream; but I knew that baby steps counted. I enrolled in a French language refresher course at the local college and planned a trip to Paris.

I wasn't ready to leave everything and move to France so I brought France home with me, turning my California coastal house into *une petite farmette*. The joke was that when the boys flew the coop, Mom got a chicken coop. I raised French hens that laid brown eggs and we ate from our organic garden to create the essence of the old French farmhouses I loved. I also took a drawing class and learned to draw those farmhouses and the Eiffel tower, which I displayed everywhere! I wrote in my journal: "If my destiny is to be in France then the path will unfold before me."

Soon after that journal entry, I met a Frenchman who made my dreams come true – or so I thought! While the relationship didn't last, and I gave up my business and *farmette*, the gift I received was a total immersion of French language and culture which intensified my love and passion for France. I fell in love with the films of Marcel Pagnol and Jacques Tati and the music of Barbara and Jacques Brel.

My trips to France continued on my own. Arriving in Paris early in the morning, getting my fix of freshly baked croissants and hitting the road in a rental car; I discovered quaint villages in the French countryside and met wonderful French women who were following their dreams making organic wines, honey and cheeses or raising

Angora goats, creating beautiful wearable art with their soft fleece. I shared their passion for keeping the artisanal ways alive.

In Paris I connected with entrepreneurs, artists and creators guiding women to find their unique style, designing *haute couture* gowns and passing down their knowledge of the very, very French *art de vivre*. While reading Colette and Georges Sand, and studying the lives of Coco Chanel and Simone de Beauvoir, I discovered French women in history and salon life during the 18th century, role models of influential *femmes*.

French women possess a style that was cultivated during the reign of King Louis XIV during the 17th century and passed down through generations. From their mothers they learn to take time for themselves, create an inviting table, and to enjoy stimulating conversation with friends and family over refined cuisine with amazing wines that could last for hours. Our young country doesn't have the same traditions and I wanted to share what I learned from the French woman and her *savoir faire*.

My desire to connect women in the US with women in France for an exchange of culture, ideas, *joie de vivre* and what it means to be feminine in today's world led to the creation of Find Your Self in France, a boutique tour design consultancy. I create custom itineraries with the intention of encouraging women to follow their dreams and reignite their passions while introducing them to my friends in France for friendship and inspiration. No matter what the language barrier, I believe we can all learn from and inspire each other.

Besides all this discovery and self-discovery, I had to return to working twelve hour days to support myself; but I continued to nurture my dreams. Cramming a full-time job and my growing travel business was stressful and again I found the courage to quit my corporate job. My sons were on their own way and I was on mine. On the day my son left for medical school, I came to Paris. Would this trip last three weeks or four months? Before the first three weeks passed, it became clear that I was going to stay longer.

Opportunities unfolded every day as I embarked on my own pilgrimage, while reading Paulo Coelho, and saying "Yes!" to life. I've stayed present to the moment and allowed the path to emerge, crisscrossing all over France, from Paris to Normandy, Burgundy to the Loire Valley, the Cote d'Azur and back to Paris again, tasting my way through each region and making lasting friendships along the way, including Dawn Bournand and the Paris Women of Success.

So many adventures later, and I am definitely a changed woman! I realized my gift as a catalyst for positive growth, connecting people to each other to make their dreams come true and fulfill their entrepreneurial spirit. I love inspiring women to take their life and business to the highest level.

I now currently live in California for the winter and then divide my time between here and France for the rest of the year to live my dream partaking of the best of both worlds in both countries. Please visit my website <u>www.FindYourSelfinFrance.com</u>.

Photo by: Claire Morris

Alecia Caine

Alecia Caine is the founder of Find Yourself In France, a boutique tour designer for women celebrating their success. As a former CPA, she has inspired hundreds of women to follow their dreams and create lasting success. After her children grew up, she reconnected with her passion for France. Having studied the language since she was 12, Alecia has also lived in Paris, and traveled extensively throughout France, while immersing herself in fashion, perfume, food and wine. She shares her passions with you ...in Paris on a fashion and beauty tour or in the French countryside tasting cheese right on a farm or having lunch on a vineyard. Learn more at: FindYourselfInFrance.com

CHAPTER 10

Paris is a Mirror of You

Olena Yashchuk Codet

I was born in Ukraine. At the time it was part of the Soviet Union, a huge country whose rulers wanted to live in their own way with the doors closed to the world outside.

I don't remember exactly where it all came from, how I started to dream about travelling and seeing that forbidden world. When I was a teenager, one of my favorite books was about the adventures of Tomek, a Polish boy who lived in the beginning of the 20th century and followed his father through all the continents. I was especially impressed by his trip to Australia. That's how my love for this and other mysterious and distant continents began.

I wrote letters to the kids of Cuba and Eastern Germany; they were on the list of "friendly" countries. I had gotten the addresses in our local "international" children's club. But my letters received no answers. So I kept searching... I spent hours in dusty libraries copying maps of Australia and making notes about the local flora and fauna.

Sometimes the gods decide to help you even with the craziest of your endeavors. When I was fifteen, the Soviet Union collapsed like an old giant of clay, destroying lives and fortunes but giving birth to something totally new, dangerous, unpredictable but very exciting.

All of a sudden, the borders started to open. My neighbors, the Jewish family we were close to, decided to move to America. We missed my neighbor's loud laughter, which we used to hear through the wall of our flat. Some of my mother's friends followed...

I remember a story my father told me about a girl who went to study in the US and how she went on to lead a successful life. It hit my imagination. I decided that one day I was going to study abroad. How and where wasn't so important.

The new life showed an ugly side to my parents' generation but it was full of unexplored possibilities for young people like me.

******

I started drawing when I was very young, in fact, as far back as I can remember. It was obvious: one day I would be a painter. Yet when I was a teenager, something happened. The magic was gone. I couldn't envision myself as an artist anymore. The end of the eighties was a tough period for my country - the end of the Soviet era. Stores were empty and our future was uncertain. I asked myself about my place in this world: what would I do with my paintings anyway?

I decided to change direction dramatically, to abandon my art studies altogether. Instead, I studied Social and Human Sciences. It was extremely interesting to learn about ancient cultures and modern languages: French and English. It helped me escape from the bleak reality that surrounded me. *My* reality was bright and full of hope. It was at about that time that I started dreaming again about studies abroad, and searching for such opportunities.

I heard about the exchange program between our university and a French institute of International Trade when I was a student at the National University "Kiev-Mohyla Academy". None of my friends knew about it until a friend of mine found out about it by chance. He and I became the first Ukrainian students to participate in this program. It was in 1996, just five years after Ukraine had declared its independence. I had no money to finance my stay in France but I did have an enormous and unstoppable desire to succeed.

Among the many miracles in my story is how I got my visa. Against all odds, I was on my way to study in Dunkirk (Dunkerque). I was only allowed to stay for three months but those three months totally, irreversibly changed my life. From there on, my personal door to the outside world was open. It was amazing, colorful, exciting. If only I could travel wherever I pleased to see more countries, to meet new people, to discover other ways of life!

For about three years I struggled. I kept looking for a way to go back to France. It became an almost obsessive dream to study there again. By the end of August 1999, I was back in Paris.

My first year was such a remarkable, intense and unforgettable experience! I think every human being should live through something similar at least once in his or her life. First, I was quite surprised to learn that some French presidents, ministers, CEOs were among the former students of the Institute of Political Studies (l'Institut d'Etudes Politiques de Paris, alias Sciences-Po), the elite school into whose prestigious Master's program I had been admitted.

Every day brought its share of new encounters and revelations… I was under the spell of the city, like millions of others before me, but this was my own, private city, my own path, these were my own discoveries. I never looked back. I immediately felt that it was a place in which I belonged.

I can't say it has always been a safe, pleasant journey, living all these years in Paris. Many have tried but not all have succeeded in getting adopted by this magnificent and capricious city. Paris took me in, though, and I found everything here that I needed: a job, a place to live, romance, beauty and love. I have lived passionate love stories; I met my husband; my first child was born here. I worked very hard to find my place under the Parisian sun.

Paris is one of those magical places that reveals your true self. It also treats you as you treat yourself. If you are a romantic, you'll find romance and beauty in every corner. If you are friendly and open-minded, you'll come across a lot of interesting and passionate people. If you are persuaded that the world is unfair, this city might be cruel and arrogant with you, a cold place… Paris is a mirror of you… It gives you the freedom to be whatever you want, but be prepared for a challenge!

If you want to feel comfortable in this country (or any country) my advice would be to learn the language and to open yourself to the culture, to let it penetrate you, nourish you, transform you. I started learning French late – when I was about eighteen years old. It seemed easy at the beginning but I found out quickly how tricky this language can be.

Back when I was still in Ukraine I remember hearing, in my French class, "Oh, Champs Elysées" the song by Joe Dassin. My heart sank and I almost cried out of despair. From that place, Paris seemed such an unattainable and distant dream. How could I possibly have imagined that by the age of twenty-four I would be living not far from Montmartre, with the Eiffel Tower framed in my window as a guest star, and the ghosts of famous artists flying around and about my neighborhood?!

******

One rainy evening, in 2002, when I was home alone, I was contemplating the majestic Parisian rooftops. All of a sudden I started drawing on an ordinary piece of paper. I could not stop, as if some supernatural force was guiding me. Hence my first series of felt-pen drawings was born. To this day they are my source of inspiration.

At the time, I had a "serious" job in the export department of a big company. It paid my bills and I could stay legally in France. It took me many long years to realize what my true vocation was. Slowly I was returning to my first passion – art.

During this period, I spent four years in London which afforded me plenty of time to reconsider my priorities. My head was full of questions: should I find a conventional and safe job, or follow my dreams? What to choose: financial security or a bold step toward the unknown?

I speak four languages, I've lived in three countries; I have two sons and one big dream – to succeed in my new mission. After having tried different professional paths, from international trade to marketing and journalism, today let me introduce to you my project as an artist.

My mission is to bring *joie de vivre*, bright colors, light and good feelings into your home or office through my artwork.

In 2009 the felt-pen cat Katou-Matou was born. He is my reincarnation into a cat's world. I'm a cat lover but, growing-up, I was never allowed to adopt one. So I decided to *create* my own. He is a lover of fine food and art; he travels from country to country, telling stories to those who adore him about the ways of life in different cultures.

Today he is in Paris or London, tomorrow in New York or Berlin. One moment, he's Magritte, another Miro or Picasso. Of course, he adores kids. He enjoys having his portrait hung in rooms. Just invite him into your home and he'll illuminate your life!

Photo by: Claire Morris

Olena Yashchuk Codet

Olena Yashchuk Codet is a French-Ukrainian artist and journalist, born in Kyiv, Ukraine, in 1976. In 1999 she moved to France. She speaks and write in 4 languages (Ukrainian, Russian, French and English). Olena has taken part in exhibitions and art fairs in both Paris and London and her drawings and paintings are in private collections in the UK, the US, France and Ukraine. Her major influences as an artist are various: Ukrainian folk art, Japanese 'estampes' Art Nouveau, photography and nature... Her favourite medium: felt-pen on paper, acrylic painting. Olena's mission is to make your life brighter! You can find her cat world creation Katou-Matou on Facebook: www. facebook.com/KatouMatou and on ETSY: www.etsy.com/fr/shop/ JoieDeVivrePaintings

—————————————————— CHAPTER 11

Seven Years

Rebecca Earley

April 2005
University of North Carolina at Chapel Hill

I'm really freaking out. Everything in my life was going normal until
yesterday. And now I have to make a decision. My French grammar
professor held me back after class to tell me that there were openings
for the Montpellier year study abroad program. He thinks that I
would be a great candidate for it, even though I would only be a
sophomore. Obviously I always planned on studying abroad in
France, but only just a semester. I mean hell, I have never been out
of the country before, and the longest time I've ever spent away from
NC was the week-long trip my brother and I took to visit our aunt in
New Mexico.

Dad always says to trust your gut. By the end of yesterday I had
decided it wasn't a good idea to go. But when I woke up this morning,
I couldn't stop thinking about how maybe this is what I've always been
waiting for. I think my gut is telling me yes...

August 2005
Charles de Gaulle airport, Paris,

I made it through two plane rides without crying, and then I found the letter from my youngest brother. The little bugger must have hidden it in my book without me noticing when we said goodbye. I have never seen him write more than two sentences in his life, and here was this two paragraph letter saying how proud of me he was, how much he will miss me, and how he knows that I made the right decision. Now I can't control my sobs. I miss my family and friends so much. I hope he is right.

November 2005
Montpellier, France

Tonight I went on my first real date! I always told myself that I would wear my hair in a ponytail on my first date, which I did. I wore the green and blue stone earrings that Mom mailed to me, and the black, sassy cardigan that my French host mom gave me. I was so nervous before he picked me up, but then everything felt right with the world as soon as we were together.

This morning was great, too. My host mom and I were having great conversation in our bathrobes over cups of tea, just as we always do. I told her that I think I will want to come back to France once this year is over. She said if I really want to, I will find a way. Luckily I don't have to worry about leaving France until another 6 months!

May 2006
Charles de Gaulle airport, Paris

Have you ever had to leave somewhere before you're ready to go? It's like someone takes your skin and bones and tells them to keep walking while the core of you is left behind. I can't get rid of the image of saying goodbye to my host mom and host brother. My host brother wouldn't stop asking me questions to prevent me from going, as seven-year-old boys do. But then it was time to go, and none of us could see one another, because our eyes were so blurry with tears.

At the airport my boyfriend watched me the whole way up the escalator until we each disappeared from view. I was the last one on the plane and had barely made it before they closed the cabin doors. I could care less, though. I was just sad.

November 2007
Viña del Mar, Chile

The transition coming back from France was much harder than expected. My psychologist suggested that I travel some more. I turned this around by convincing my dad that the only way I could complete my French and Spanish majors, and be fluent in both languages, would be to live abroad again. So here I am, sitting on the edge of the freezing, rough Pacific Ocean with my feet dangling in the water, my third month into my study abroad program in Chile. My travel mind is happy, and I am head over heels in love with a Chilean, but there is still a part of me that keeps thinking about France...

March 2008
University of North Carolina at Chapel Hill

I had been waiting for the phone call since 8am this morning. I kept my phone in my hand during class, in the event that it might ring. It finally did just as I was on the brick path heading back to my apartment. I started to jump up and down and scream silently inside when I heard the sentence I was hoping for: "We are offering you a job in advertising in New York City."

March 2011
Lago de Atitlán, Guatemala

Today I had an epiphany in the middle of Lago de Atitlán in Guatemala. This has been my first trip abroad since moving to NYC. The adventures, the beauty, and living in another language awakened a part of me that had been dormant since I left Chile and France. My epiphany happened in a tiny row boat, in the middle of the lake, surrounded by volcanoes. I realized that if I'm ever going to move back to France, I have to do it now, and I cannot give up until I finally do.

July 2011
Paris, France

It's my last day in Paris after 5 days of interviews. None of the companies have openings. I walked the streets by myself, past the Louvre, from the 1st to the 2nd arrondissements, crying silently knowing that my dream was not going to come true. I stopped at a café for a glass of wine, and the waiter asked me why I was sad. I told him that I wanted to move to Paris, but I was failing. He looked me in the eyes and said, "I know you will be back. You belong here."

October 2011
Brooklyn, New York

I just hung up the phone on my mom. She won't stop asking me if I have any news from the companies I interviewed with in Paris. Everyone else has given up on me moving to Paris, so why doesn't she? Can't she understand that maybe settling down, getting married and starting a family is the way that life is supposed to be? Maybe following your dreams cannot always happen? At least that's what I'm trying to tell myself. The truth is I just don't have the courage to tell her that I have given up, too...

Friday, January 13, 2012
New York, New York

OH. MY. GOSH!!! THE HEAD OF THE DATA DEPARTMENT AT OGILVY PARIS JUST FOUND THE HARD COPY OF MY RESUME AND CONTACTED ME ON LINKEDIN!!! THEY HAVE AN OPENING!!! THEY WANT TO KNOW IF I'M INTERESTED!!! THIS IS IT!! THIS IS IT!!! Please, don't let me screw this up...

February 2012
Chapel Hill, North Carolina

I am popping champagne with my mom, dad, brother, and best friend in the same place that it all started 7 years ago... I JUST GOT A JOB OFFER TO MOVE TO FRANCE!!!!

August 2012
John F. Kennedy airport, New York City

Well, here I am in JFK, getting ready to board my first ever one-way flight. It only now starts to hit me what this all really means. Fuck.

August 2012
Charles de Gaulle airport, Paris

After I boarded the flight, I felt the weight lift off my shoulders as the wheels of the plane no longer touched the US. I fell asleep and woke up with a thud as the plane landed itself in France with the pink sunrise peeking out of the cloudy sky. The fear and anxiety I felt in JFK began to melt away. I was finally home.

Epilogue

November 2013
Paris, France

Here I am one year later, in my studio apartment in Saint-Germain-des-Prés. People ask me all the time how long I will be here, and what is next. The truth is that I don't know the answer yet, but I'm finding bits of pieces of it every day. It's in the boulangerie on rue de Rennes. It's in the reflection of the Seine when the City of Lights is lit up at night. It's in the eyes of the new friends, and in the smiles of old ones. The most amazing part is realizing that it's just the beginning. It's the beginning of a new life in which I am finally my full self. The only thing that matters now is never losing the spark inside of me that Paris has finally set free.

Photo: Author's personal collection

Rebecca Earley

Rebecca Earley was born in Chicago, Illinois in 1986, but she likes to call North Carolina, where she spent the majority of her childhood, her home. She graduated from the University of North Carolina at Chapel Hill in 2008, with a double major in French and in Spanish. Following graduation she spent four years in New York City, working in advertising and living in Brooklyn. She now lives in Paris working for the global advertising firm, Ogilvy, where she is finally living her dream.

———————— CHAPTER 12

Paris Became My Creative Playground

Petronela Zainuddin

I am kind of an unusual Parisian and you are about to discover why. I am a left-handed young woman with green eyes and blond hair. No, I am not Norwegian nor Russian. I am Slovak, like Adriana Karembeu. I came to Paris thanks to a nonprofit organization, fell in love with the city, left it for nine months then came back. I learned French in three years, married a man from Madagascar and became a creative entrepreneur.

But let's start from the beginning.

My grandma was born in France and when she was eight her family returned to Slovakia. I think that coming to Paris was my destiny. In 2005 I started a one year assignment as vice-president for the AIESEC Exchange Program in France. It took me eleven months to realize that I had found the man of my life and he was sitting right next to me. Karim was my colleague, my roommate and my best friend in Paris. By the time I realized that we belonged together, my assignment was almost over and I had to go back to Slovakia.

I returned to Paris in 2007 when I got accepted for an HR internship with a large American car component manufacturer. The funny thing was that the year before I had worked with this company and the position that I ended up getting was created based on a proposal I had written!

When my internship was nearing the end I started to look for a job. I was dedicated and I knew what I wanted: an amazing job in strategy consulting. Despite the facts that my French was still not fluent, I didn't have a degree from a prestigious French business school and I needed a work permit, I remained positive. After a few months of endless job applications, a failed interview at BCG and refusals from other consulting firms, I talked to the Global HR manager in our company. I got the opportunity to become Sales Planning Analyst but the condition was that I had to relocate to Germany.

I said NO.

Surprisingly I got the job anyway and the bonus was I was based in Paris! My dream had come true and nothing and nobody could stop me on my way to happyland. But my happiness did not last very long. In September 2008 the financial crisis hit our company and changed forever our way of doing business. My strategic role turned into one of endless 'number crunching' of sales forecasts. After four months in the job I wanted to quit. I ended up staying four more years.

The problem was somewhere else. As I mentioned earlier, I am left-handed and when I was little I attended art school for eight years. Now imagine what happens when you lock a creative mind into a financial job. It's an explosion. I started to compensate for my job frustration with numerous creative projects in my free time. Paris became my creative playground.

First I discovered mosaic art at the "Salon de la Creation & Savoir Faire", organized each November at Porte de Versailles. Then I found "Championnet Carrelages", the amazing tile shop located in the 18th district of Paris. Each time I went there I ended up spending at least one hour and €100 and would create things like mosaic pictureframes, bed trays or a mosaic coffee table.

Then I started experimenting with photography. My husband and I organized a Photo Marathon in the "Le Marais" neighborhood. This contest had very specific rules and a time deadline for submitting work on topics like "Chinese in the Street", "Happy People" or "Sleeping Beauty".

One day I saw the movie "Yes Man" in which Zooey Deschanel and a group of people take pictures while jogging in the morning; so I took my reflex camera, sat on a Vélib bike (rental bikes located throughout the city) and started to take pictures of Paris while biking. I went to the Eiffel Tower, the Champs-Élysées, rode the streets of Saint-Germain, Odéon, Saint-Michel and Châtelet. It was dangerous, exciting and my photos were great.

My mind was full of ideas and my heart was full of feelings since I had come back to Paris. I started to blog about different topics... Life in Paris, Creative Liberation and even Positive Leadership. I was writing more for myself than for others. I invented the TIWI concept (Today I Was Inspired) and started to capture hundreds of inspiring moments, places and ideas like:

- a homeless person fishing for money in front of the cinema close to Opera
- kids steering small boats in the fountain of Tuileries Gardens
- discovering Paris with a tour guide on bicycle
- finding inspiring books at museum bookshops
- walking through the "Passages Parisiens" on a rainy day
  ...and many more.

I tried to keep my mind and my hands busy all the time. When I was not taking pictures of Paris streets, writing blogs or doing mosaic, I started to paint. During one sunny Saturday we were walking from Place de la République to Bastille. There I saw it: a three floor shop with art materials called Rougier & Plé. When I entered my heart was singing. It was full of notebooks, markers, brushes, oil and water colors, canvas, scrapbook papers and everything you need to release your imagination. I could create even more.

But no matter how much creativity I experienced in my free time, my job was killing me. It was not the company, not the team or my boss. In fact I had great bosses. The first one was always positive and looking at the bright side of problems and the second one was caring and even sent me to a training course on "How to facilitate creativity workshops". The seminar was run by a well-known French training company but it was a disaster. I was bored and disappointed and I told myself there <u>must be a better way</u> to develop creative thinking in others.

My entrepreneurial journey started in 2010. After many months of reflection I read a book that changed my life: "The Future of Management" by Gary Hamel. It was a call for dreamers and doers and I decided to become a pioneer in creativity education. On the 10th of May my husband and I officially launched Good Morning Creativity. At the beginning it was just a blog about techniques and methods in creative thinking, but people started to read it and began asking for more articles.

At the beginning it seemed imPOSSIBLE to make a business out of this idea. We had no portfolio of services, no clients, no references and I had no Masters degree in Creativity! This was entirely new territory for us as well as for companies, for society, for Paris. Although many people started to promote innovation as the best way to get out of a crisis, no one really knew how to foster creative thinking within their teams.

Meanwhile, I applied for a new job in a consulting company trying to develop their leadership programs portfolio. When I presented Good Morning Creativity, they were ready to hire me if I sold the project to them and developed it in-house. I took this as the sign to move forward, register the brand and set up the company with my husband instead.

A few months later we were called for our first consulting mission. We designed and ran a creativity workshop for two start-up teams merging together and looking for a new name. We started with bringing chocolate and when people said, "It is Ramadan, we can't eat", I knew that it was going to be fun! They had a small cat who jumped and hung on our trousers while we were trying to do our training. Despite the challenges and stress from the first project, we helped them to find a great name: "Smart & Geek".

One year later, Good Morning Creativity was awarded as the "International Start-up of the Year 2011" at the ISUM conference in Paris. This reward encouraged us to continue and invent new experiential workshops, creative LABs, doodling seminars and new thinking methods for teams and their leaders. Since we first started, we have realized more than seventy projects and trained over 2000 people in six different countries. Today we continue to develop creative managers, creative women, creative educators and creative kids.

Since we are all foreigners, Good Morning Creativity became a pioneer of creativity education in English in Paris! This quickly became our unique trademark and many companies, business schools, chambers of commerce and prestigious conference organizers started to contact us for a variety of international projects in Paris. Our future ambition is to launch Creative Leaders Expeditions for foreigners and international groups and make Paris the world's leading reference for creativity development.

I still remember the moment back in 2003 when I wrote on a piece of paper my strengths and weaknesses. I wrote that I am NOT creative, because I was not able to improvise and come up with ideas in front of other people! Today I manage my own creative business in Paris, I try to democratize creative techniques through my visual blog "365 Creativity Facilitators" and every day I help managers and their teams to be more creative at work. I have literally transformed my life and invented my own job. And you can do the same!

Start your own creative life: dream, question and experiment. Buy a small notebook for your TIWI moments, question status quo, try new ideas and find sponsors for your projects. But most importantly, do what you LOVE to do.

Photo: WikiStage ESCP Europe, Juraj Bartoš
and author's personal collection

Petronela Zainuddin

Petronela Zainuddin is a creative mind, passionate about leadership and education. She is founder of Good Morning Creativity, an award winning, learning company based in Paris. She works with clients all over Europe to blend business strategy, experiential learning and creativity. She is an international speaker and the author of the 365 Creativity Facilitators visual blog. www.goodmorningcreativity.com

CHAPTER 13

From Dream to Reality

Geneviève Prono

My first memory of Paris is with my mother in the Metro. I'm not yet five. We are waiting for the next train to enter the station. I have a book in my hands: a very precious book. I feel so proud and excited. It's wrapped inside a yellow plastic bag which has large black letters on it. I've been told these letters are the name of the store where the book has been bought: Gilbert Jeune. On our way to a doctor's appointment, we have stopped at this famous bookstore in the "Quartier Latin." It sells used books as well as new ones on every subject, from school and textbooks to novels and nonfiction. It's busy and bustling. We are surrounded by the students of the nearby universities and schools, rushing around with piles of books in their hands. That's when my mother had the inspiration to offer me a reading manual.

For the moment she still acts as a translator, telling me: "On that sign is the name of the station: Saint Michel. And here is the direction we are heading to: Porte d'Orléans". But very soon, I will no longer need her help, it's a promise. I will be able to master the art of making sense of the groups of letters that are everywhere in Paris: on the walls of the Metro, on the side of the buses, on the large green lamp posts with their advertisements for plays and concerts, on the newspaper kiosks. A whole new world is opening up for me. My love for the written word as well as my love for Paris is beginning right here.

Years have passed, I am now sixteen. My family has moved back to Paris after several years in the States and in another part of France. I have never stopped reading since the secret behind the letters was revealed to me. The magic is there every time I open a book and I have decided I want to create magic too. Play with words. Tell a story. Be a writer, a published author.

I look for inspiration. Words come in easily. I like to put them on paper and play with them. But what about the story, the message brought by the words? What should I write about? I have tried out poems, short stories, just jotting down impressions and feelings. But I'm not satisfied. And the question follows me as I walk my way through the streets of Paris, following the footsteps of some of my favorite authors.

I often wander off between the fifteenth arrondissement around Montparnasse, up rue de Rennes to Saint Germain des Près in the sixth arrondissement or through the Luxembourg gardens to the fifth, reaching Odéon and the Saint Michel fountain, near the Seine River. If the weather is nice I sit on a bench to read or write or watch the passers-by and the street artists.

There is so much to look at, to smell, to listen to, to feel and taste. Paris sharpens all my senses: the colors of the markets and the shops in the little streets; the busy noise of the city: horns of cars and bells of bicycles, the glimpses of conversations in various languages; the smells from the cosmopolitan restaurants: Greek, Chinese, Lebanese...

When it's colder I take refuge in obscure or famous cafés, sensing the shadows of past writers, artists and intellectuals, hoping maybe some of their talent might rub off on me. I can stay hours in their places of predilection, such as Café de Flore and Les Deux Magots in Saint Germain des Près, reading the books of those who have influenced my thoughts and reflection: Simone de Beauvoir, Jean-Paul Sartre, Ernest Hemingway, Guy de Maupassant... I try to write. I do some journaling, lost in my thoughts and dreams. Or I let myself be distracted by what's happening around me and try to sketch with words what I see. It's the waiter in his black dress coat and wide white apron, going swiftly around the tables, taking orders, handling large trays full of tiny white cups filled with steaming dark black coffee, heavy pots of tea, glasses of wine or pastis. My eyes go from the old lady wearing her jewels with the dignity of the past, to the couple flirting and obviously in love, to the business man reading his newspaper or the group of students immersed in a heated discussion… I try to imagine their lives, their thoughts. I come to realize I lack experience, the experience of life… I need to live before I can really write.

Time has passed again. I am now a grown-up woman of thirty. I have been away from Paris, living in various places: the north of France, Iraq, and back. My unfinished manuscripts are in a box somewhere with my diaries, somewhat forgotten. I'm busy with life. I am married and pregnant with my third child. I'm in the doctor's office battling because I want to avoid a third cesarean. My heart is full of sorrow: my mother has died a few weeks ago from brain cancer. I feel alone. Paris and books have let me down. This time I haven't found the right read to help me as I usually do when I need answers to my questions.

The cesarean has been done, bringing me to a merciful anger that will pull me out of my sorrow. I will not give up. I will have the large family of my dreams and birth naturally … and I will write the book I have been searching for the past year and have not found. I realize that this is what I have been meant to write. Not a novel or poetry or even an essay but a guide, for women like me, trying to make sense of their body and the birthing practices. I call for testimonies, do interviews, read books on how to write and publish nonfiction. I go back to school to learn everything I can. I attend meetings on home and natural childbirth. I follow every lead I have, running through Paris from one place to another with my little one in a sling.

It's time to approach publishers. I have selected a few that target women's issues. I send them a well-crafted proposal and wait. Answers come back one at a time. Some - the majority – are just not interested.

Others like my style and/or the subject but... they consider the number of women who would buy the book too low to publish it!

I'm very disappointed of course. But by now, I'm pregnant with my fourth child. And finally all I did has helped me immensely: I will give birth to this child naturally before I leave Paris again to live in Saudi Arabia.

And now, I'm once more busy with my life, discovering a new country and coping with its rules, having two more children without cesarean or epidural, thus fulfilling my dream of six children. And the manuscript follows the others into a box. I will just put it on hold. Some day, I tell myself...

Years have passed. Many busy years, helping women overcome their cesarean and prepare for another birth, going back to school to study psychology, leading workshops on interpersonal communication, working in the corporate world in a training department, leaving that company to start my own business, going through a separation and starting a new life while taking care of my children who are growing up fast.

Women have been asking for my book all these years. A publisher has even approached me interested in the subject. Is it time to dig out my manuscript? I have changed. I'm another woman now. The book would have to be rewritten. My approach is different from all that I have learned and lived. And mostly I have fallen in love again, giving a lot of time to a passion witnessed by Paris and its streets, where we walk endlessly hand-in-hand in awe with all the treasures we find: old shops in small streets, beautiful inside gardens, cozy restaurants...

Six more years have passed. I have ended my relationship and I am now ready to move on to my next life. It is time to finish writing that book and publish it. I have tried myself out with some chapters in collective books, as a start; enough to already have an author page on Amazon. I'm well under way with my manuscript, both in English and in French.

My dream is becoming a reality. I have gained experience, that life experience I felt I was lacking at sixteen. I have a plethora of subjects to write about now. Stories to tell. Messages to share. Thank you, Paris, for serving as a checking point all those years, a place where I have been able to regroup, live, love, learn and leap to who I am today.

Photo by: Claire Morris

Geneviève Prono

Psychotherapist, coach, holistic healer, speaker, facilitator, trainer, author, Geneviève Prono has been helping women and men for 25 years at key moments of their life and during periods of transition and change like pregnancy, entering parenthood, separations, traumatic experiences or changes of orientation. She also trains and coaches health professionals, social workers and alternative professionals and has been doing that for fifteen years. She started her own company in 2002: Chrysalide France http://www.chrysalidefrance.com

CHAPTER 14

The Beginning of a New Life

Françoise Bor De Ley

To briefly introduce myself, my name is Françoise Bor De Ley, I was born on 20th July 1980 in Strasbourg and I am now fortunate to have a great husband and three beautiful boys.

The part of my life that I want to talk about begins on 27th September 2003, the day of the birth of my eldest son.

"What significance does this have?" you may be asking. For me, this day marks the beginning of a new life and new projects. When my eldest son was born, I was still in school; I was forced to reorganize my life. I had to approach the problem from another angle: "What can I study while working, making time for my husband and raising my son?"

So I started evening classes in real estate law at the CNAM. This was not my first choice (which had been Faculty of Science and Applied Foreign Languages) but it allowed me to continue to grow. During these three years of study I also had to deal with the repercussions of medical errors, which led me to having to undergo three major operations, one of which (posing an abdominal plate) compromised any future pregnancy. It is when we lose our health that we realize its importance.

Illness is the only thing that can make everything impossible, unlike the rest of the usual life concerns (financial, relationship, work ...). Thus, after this painful period, which lasted nearly a year and a half, my husband and I placed our bets on expanding our family and thwarting fate.

It turned out to be a successful challenge which allowed us to be parents for the second time. Then my husband found a job elsewhere and we had to move; so I found myself unable to continue my evening classes.

It was time for my desire to set up and create my own company to come to life. I started working on the project with a consultant. The idea was to create a company of real estate hunters, based in Paris in an ideal central location with exceptional VIP services and exclusively reserved for foreign investors.

As I continued on this path, I managed to obtain recognition of my previous studies in the third year of the Faculty of Law; this gave me the business card qualifications I needed for my personal project.

I returned to the faculty bench at the age of 30, determined to succeed. But it was without counting on fate's ability to thwart my plans; just two months later I became pregnant again. I will never forget that one night when we were having friends to dinner, and for me, everything came crashing down in an instant. I knew what it meant: I would not be able to continue my course work nor my project, on which I had worked so hard for two years.

Being a mom who should not have more children, it was obvious that my pregnancy would be a priority. This would be complex and risky. I had to start from scratch and once again take the problem from another angle: "What could I study, mostly from a distance (as I would be bedridden for several months of my pregnancy) that would allow me to continue my project to create my own business?"

After a long period of research, I happened upon a design school (Interior Decoration) based in Paris, offering distance learning courses and workshops that would lead to a degree in interior design.

This was an area opposite to what I had studied before, but it touched an old passion: drawing. Since my childhood, I had studied drawing.

The next problem was that the program required a "bac + two" (two years of undergraduate studies) in Fine Arts, which I obviously did not have. After various negotiations with the school's administration, they agreed to consider my application (sketches and paintings I had made) and required me to pass a few tests. I came out "triumphant" and I was given permission to start the training.

It was a revelation for me! I loved what I studied, what I learned, what I saw. After thirty years I had finally found my way and I could say "thank you" to my son for this path which, though sometimes chaotic, was so beneficial.

Thus, after two years of intensive training, I created my interior design company based in Paris and named it: "De Montigny Decoration & Design". I also discovered the tax and legal maze of a small business in France.

A recurring question from most people I meet is: "Why that name?" and "Why Paris?" I wanted to give a family dimension to my work, which is why I chose to incorporate the name "De Montigny." It had belonged to my ancestors, and for me, it gave a "special" and unique air to my company. As for Paris, for me it was an obvious choice! The capital of France: taste, fashion, luxury, history, architecture ... it was the perfect place!

The adventure began... After several trips to Milan, the Italian capital of design and fashion, I decided to work exclusively with Italian suppliers. Then, as I was reviewing my business and studying various options to change, the idea of an association came to me. I studied the idea for a while and finally decided it was worth pursuing. I was introduced to various people, each of whom, as time passed, always wanted to significantly change my company. It was then that I met a woman, also an entrepreneur, who was in search of a new direction and who was equally passionate about design.

After months of reorganization work (from my side only, since she was still operating in her own company role) I organized a decisive meeting with my potential partner and my accountants to define our future business operations.

Unfortunately, this alliance ultimately proved disastrous. The woman wanted 90% of the stakes in the company, while I was the only one who would be providing guarantors, the company name, the work I had done and the skills I contributed. This filled me with disappointment. I immediately stopped the negotiations and was left with the unpleasant impression of starting over from scratch along with having lost many months of work.

And so, I am alone on the entrepreneurial path once again. Fortunately, I'm lucky to have my good friend Sandrine P., "wedding planner of talent" in Paris, with whom I work a lot. We support each other in our respective businesses and it is through her that I came to know the wonderful group "Paris Women of Success".

Being a woman can already complicate things from a professional point of view, often making it doubly difficult to prove ourselves. As for the woman who wants to create her own company, it becomes a real obstacle course. The support is not always there, even though it is in these moments of doubt that we need it the most.

As of today, I am taking the idea that I had originally proposed for creating an association and will try to develop it on my own. The task seems insurmountable to me some days, but I still continue to believe.

So, on the advice of my accountants, I filed three other brands, allowing me to diversify my business. My main company, "De Montigny Deco & Design," will be assigned to my national interior design projects, and a second brand will be allocated to large-scale projects based abroad.

Meanwhile, I want to open an e-shop that offers decorative items, art paintings, unique designs, and custom furniture, which will, for the most part be created by young designers, discovered during my travels. It's important for me to give back the help I myself have enjoyed in my life.

I believe we must give life to the projects that are important to us, those we are tempted to put off to "another day"; every day counts. We must therefore remain conscious and always take care of ourselves, too. I have finally decided to make some of my dreams come true. For me, we must give back what life gives us, so that balance is maintained.

Another personal passion, namely photography, is beginning to take on life. In fact, I am currently training as a photographer. Since I never do enough for my taste, I have also signed up for a third year of training in interior design, which will allow me to get my Bachelors with a specialization in landscape architecture.

As you can see the road is still long for me (finish my two areas of study – photography and interior design, create and develop my other brands, find new investors, develop new client relationships…) but I believe, in spite of everything and above all else, that Paris – this beautiful city – is the cradle for all ideas to come to life, and God willing even more new beginnings in the coming years.

If I chose to tell my story, it is to encourage other women to believe in your dreams and no matter what pitfalls you meet, to persevere for yourself, your balance, and your life; and to surround yourself with those who can help you.

Photo: Author's personal collection

Françoise Bor De Ley

Françoise Bor De Ley, 33 years old, is married and mother of three boys. Born in Strasbourg, the "Capital of Europe", she was raised in a Franco-German culture and speaks several languages. Though Françoise holds degrees in Languages and Real Estate Law, she has returned to her first passion : Art. She found her calling in Interior Design and graduated from the "Interior Deco" School in Paris. Françoise founded the "DeMontigny Group" which she launched in January 2014, offering services in: Interior and Landscape design, Works of Art, Furniture, and Photography. Readers receive a free one hour consultation as part of a service offered by the De Montigny Group. www.de-montigny-group.com

CHAPTER 15

A Letter to My Child

Sanda Taranu

My love,

If I were to pass anything on to you, I would tell you this: be confident but humble, follow your instinct, don't quit your dreams, and see that what you do matters. Don't let yourself be convinced into why it couldn't be done. Things may get complicated and difficult at times; people may let you down, and keep you down even with the best of intentions. Get up, get out and pave your path.

Know that your instinct is God guiding you and pray when in doubt.

I have changed a lot since I was seventeen, and yet I have not changed much. I was the most determined girl I knew back then, and I had one dream: to be a fashion designer – not something to be taken seriously in Romania at the time. So I went to Law school and started on my way to becoming a notary. One year later I decided to go to Chicago - not because I didn't like law, but just because… I felt I needed to try this "magical" country everyone but me was dreaming about. I remember packing things Mom would take out saying, "You're only going for two months!" I realize now how I scared her, what I must have put her through.

Ten years later I was still there, changing jobs and attending classes. I felt so fortunate when I got into a fashion design school! Yet by the time I got my designer degree I had lost my designer motivation.

More years passed by in a blur before I met my French man, a change oh so very welcomed and back to Europe I came, armed with a chance for a new life. Soon after the initial excitement of the different and the wonderful wore off, the new life took over without friends or the independence I was so accustomed to. In the following years I continued to add to an image of myself I felt I still needed to polish.

So many saw this journey as incredible and courageous, an "I could never do that" kind of thing. I took everything as normal never thinking of it "plus que ça", as the French would say. Searching for myself lost somewhere in translation, needing to find my sense of belonging; I guess big moves can do that to you. I did, on the other hand come to realize the world is not so inconceivably big and mysteriously unknown after all; countries become cities, friends become families.

I never thought I would settle on France, and love it. As weird as it feels thinking about it now, those pictures I would stare at in the Merchandise Mart, those old stone houses with colored storefronts and narrow streets, flowers in the sun and an air of a charmed lost world which never-the-less was so alive, those pictures reflected the dream place where we are now! The all-charming France. Your instincts and your dreams are your projected future, believe in them.

Now, twenty years later, I am gathering the rocks to build that little countryside road into a highway. I've finally made the decision not to listen to well-intentioned people giving me cautious advice, nor let insecurities win over my heart any more. No more taking other people's opinions of my capabilities personally, continuing to respect them nonetheless. And that, my love, that was not easy. Ready to accept myself, look calmly at all the failures and successes I've experienced, and move forward, slowly and surely. Not far behind are the times when I would pause to wonder what my life would have looked like had I never set out in the first place. I know now that not following my instinct would have chased me forever, and I have made peace with myself.

I've realized and accepted my purpose: let this artist, entrepreneur, dinosaur, woman get out and express herself and do something worthy with that expression, no matter where I landed in this world. I suppose I had to get here the way I did in order to fully mature my vision: I want to be remembered not for my designs but for my impact on someone's life, I want to feel what I do matters. And that, my love, that is what I want to pass on to you.

You had to come, so I could start growing. Ever since you came I have developed a high sensibility towards children. Seeing you so fragile, so helpless, so small and pretty like a "croissant chaud", as Papa would say, and seeing in parallel the stories of other children who cannot taste what you can - not even a mother's love - that is something that is continuing to mark me. I hope that by being great at what I do as a designer I will be able to translate it into a greater undertaking towards those other children, and that you will want to join me.

Ah, and let's not forget Paris! How envied we are just for being here. As much as I love Chicago, I, for one, couldn't wait to move. The myth of Paris, France, old Europe and the adventure of a new beginning, a new life I could invent and mold anyway I wanted! Take one! The city in itself is constant motivation, inspiration, so rich in culture it feels like history will spill out of those countless statues' mouths. You almost expect to hear Edith Piaff singing "Je ne regrette rien" while sipping red wine at a corner restaurant on a summer evening (which we did, except it was her perfect double - still priceless). The thought of a fresh buttery croissant is enough to make you want to get up in the morning, and I'm still determined to try all the different pastries in the "boulangerie", as soon as I have had enough of the same ones.

Of course there's also the Paris with its sad faced Metro travelers and bad service, but well, it's still Paris. My favorites are the "balades" in the spring, reminding me of those walks when I was pregnant with you and had nothing to do but get lost and discover Paris in all its magic for both of us. I like to think I came here to wait for you in the best of settings.

Hosting friends, over time, I noticed some manage to get to appreciate the city, while some don't. I try to pass on my excitement for what I like to think are my discoveries here: a small Spanish-like square with a "boulangerie" displaying an art deco painted tile wall across a charming old church, and one street further an amazing bridal boutique where I attempted to try a dress on before my wedding (and didn't manage to because the first thing the owner asked was my budget; even if I lied, the dress in the display was more than I could have imagined!).

I find myself repeating the same stories, with the same excitement as if I had just discovered them. I find myself lost in contemplation of the same buildings, same details, and same smells. I insist on putting myself in a place from which I can continuously be reminded of the beauty of the sights and my gratitude for what has been given to me. It is easy to take things for granted. It is dangerous to take things for granted.

Be grateful for the gift of smelling the roses and be kind to people even if they aren't kind to you. Oh, that takes a lot of years of practice and I'm still working on it. Be you and don't second-guess yourself like I did at times. Be a person of your word, a person stepping on her word is not worth being around. Guard your mouth, it is your words that will lead you or haunt you. Even if I have always known that, I have not always managed to live it. Self control is the key to grace, and grace, my love, grace is what this life is all about. Had I realized this sooner, your second name would have been Grace.

I like to think one day you'll be by my side in reaching out through this undertaking. I like to think this will be your legacy, too. As much as this is my project, my passion, I cannot not think of you as a part of it.

After all and out of all, it is you who are my greatest adventure.

Mama

Photo: Author's personal collection

Sanda Taranu

Born in Timisoara, Romania in 1976, Sanda lived in Chicago most of her adult life before the next big move to Paris. After graduating from a Fashion design school and making various stops in RE, property management and English teaching she decided on a great undertaking: more than just fashion, a fashion design and lifestyle boutique with a parallel focus on the 'other' children. Sanda is mother to a princess and wife to a French man.

Dramatic yet simple, timeless and unique, her pieces address that strong and classy "Jacqueline of all trades" who knows life does not have to be perfect to be wonderful. And who cares. www.atelier-52. com, St@atelier-52.com"

To know that just one life has breathed easier because you lived, that is to have succeeded.

-RW Emerson

CHAPTER 16

Rebirth

Celine Douay

I was reborn on May 17, 2013 in Paris, on a sunny day. For the first time in my life I experienced a feeling of happiness, fulfillment and harmony between my body and soul. I would like to share with you some vignettes from my life, to show you how Paris has transformed it.

For years I lived in a reality that was not mine. I studied in several French cities, including one year in Paris; that year left me with a bitter taste. For me, Paris meant dirt, insecurity and poverty. I often said, "When you get to Paris alone, you leave alone". That is the reason I decided to start my career in London. London seemed to me to be an energizing, cosmopolitan, warm city where everything is possible.

In 2006 I left France with £350 in my pocket and no job. My plan was to stay with my cousin for a few weeks while I looked for work. I was fortunate to get a very nice position in the online industry and I grew up professionally in an American company based in London.

Within a few years I had been promoted several times and became European Sales Manager with many responsibilities. I earned a comfortable living and I enjoyed the work environment, the values of respect, meritocracy and the spirit of winning. I was delighted with the culture of the company; I met some great people and made very good friends.

In my heart, however, a lack manifested without my being able to name it. I felt the need to help people, to develop their potential and guide them to achieve their goals. I decided to study at The Coaching Academy while I continued to work and did this for two years. In the meantime I met a wonderful man and we decided to live together. I have always had a passion for travelling and it turned out he did, too. We discovered many countries together and even talked about eventually starting a family.

December 2011 was the beginning of a long period of tragedy for me. Something was missing in my work so I decided to leave my comfort zone and signed a contract with a French company, still working in London. It offered me a hefty salary increase. I left my beloved environment with a heavy heart but I wanted a new challenge. You know how sometimes you change something in your life without thinking twice? That is exactly what I did.

I was constantly looking to improve my performance, my productivity, trying to be the best. In a very short time my life turned into a nightmare. I realized there was a huge difference between working for the Americans and working for the French. I did not find myself in the French model. I gave body and soul to the French company hoping to establish a sustainable subsidiary in the UK. Stress played tricks on me without my realizing it. My body sent me messages that I did not listen to.

In June 2012 I lost my job without any notice; the director decided to close down the UK office – we were not competitive enough for the market. My ego suffered greatly from the decision. Despite my project of an around-the-world trip I became unbearable for my boyfriend. I choked him without even realizing it; indirectly, he was paying for my unhappiness.

Then in July 2012 I almost died eating a peach! I had an angioedema; fortunately the hospital was close, which avoided it being fatal. I am still shocked about this episode of my life and I become paranoid with all summer fruit and other delicacies. I had never had a single food allergy before.

In August 2012 my sweetheart woke up beside me and told me it was over. It seemed to me like his feelings had disappeared overnight. It's hard for me to explain the pain I felt that day, there is no word to describe the sensation. Cries came out of my throat as I had never heard. My tears haven't stopped flowing. My world, my dreams collapsed one after the other – I even thought I was cursed.

I needed to move out of the apartment I shared with him and I had no work; it was impossible for me to stay any longer. I needed to be surrounded by my family. Four days later I decided to put all my things in storage and I returned to France after seven years abroad.

I was not psychologically prepared for this. I had been planning to return to France in my old age, not before I was sixty years old! My sense of inadequacy made me feel like I was a stranger in my own country. I experienced real culture shock.

My family tried to comfort me but I was not receptive anymore and I thought that we were no longer on the same wavelength. I had the impression of being pushed down even deeper rather than being supported.

Also in August 2012, my grandmother went to hospital after a bad fall which left her virtually dead for twenty-four hours. A blood clot had traveled to her brain and left her as a vegetable in a hospital bed, when she had always been an energetic and talkative woman.

I write this passage of my life with sadness and deep revolt. What else could happen to me? Almost every area of my life had been devastated by this storm of events.

I felt lonely; I realized I was not a child anymore: I was a woman who had to take responsibility for herself. I felt drained, I did not recognize myself. In the mornings I would often awaken with the sensation of being sucked up by my bed, or with a heavy weight pushing on me, or heart palpitations, dizziness, or anxiety attacks ...

In this situation you can choose to fight it or ditch it. I decided not to let myself down. We are partly responsible for what happens to us, playing the role of the victim would not have helped me.

I had the feeling of having been ripped out of London and then thrown violently back into Paris without any sense of direction. I began to question myself. Why did I lose all my points of reference? Could someone show me the right direction?

By an incredible stroke of luck my best friend from childhood, Thomas, and a good friend, Jeremy, offered to let me stay with them in their large apartment in Paris. I will never be able to thank them enough for what they did for me. I have a long list of friends to say thank you to for taking care of me during this hard time. They have given me the strength to persevere. And even though my parents were very awkward through all of this, I realized that they, too, tried to help as they could.

In October 2012 I decided to surround myself with many professionals, like my doctor who told me to avoid taking antidepressants. By word of mouth, I was introduced to energy therapists, psychologists, a sophrologist, a nutritionist, personal, professional and spiritual coaches. Paris brought me many wonderful encounters with people who have given me a lot of love and messages of hope.

Fate has forced me to pause and take time to rebuild myself in order to find my inner self, welcome my true nature, and understand the lack that haunted me for years. I decided to listen to my body, be guided by my intuition, and believe in the future. Nietzsche was right, "Anything that does not kill you makes you stronger".

Since I was a child I have enjoyed singing. I decided to take lessons in order to record a few titles in the near future. I think it is important to ask yourself, what did you enjoy doing when you were a kid? How do you feel thinking about that?

I do not want to repeat my mistakes, so I decided to follow what seems to be my mission: helping others. I chose to become an entrepreneur and launched my own company, GoForCoaching! I have several years of experience in business and marketing which helps me understand different problems in the sales environment. I help people in their personal life to get over their beliefs and limitations to reach their goals. It makes me feel good when I see my clients satisfied at the end of each session.

It is essential to have a solid foundation in order to create a stable life. To find my balance and myself it was necessary for me to return to my roots. After nine months, I have been able to get my head above water; it is like carrying a pregnancy to term and giving birth to myself.

Paris gave me the opportunity to find myself. For that I will always be grateful!

Photo: Author's personal collection

Céline Douay

Multiculturally influenced, CélineDouay is a mentor, personal life and business coach. Born in 1981 in Versailles, Céline's open minded soul encouraged her to travel around the world and speak different languages. (French, English, German, Arabic). After working 7 years in online marketing management on a European level, she decided to launch her own business helping individuals and entrepreneurs to achieve their goals and live in their true nature by using creative tools based on her extra-sensorial perceptions and analyzing capabilities. Certified from The Coaching Academy in London, she is accredited for many psycho metrics tools such as DISC and NLP. www. goforcoaching.com, celine@goforcoaching.com

CHAPTER 17

The Making of Patricia Parisienne
Patricia Rosas

I hurried off the plane, excited to see my new nephew, sister, and *beauf* (French nickname for my brother-in-law, short for *beau-frère*). It had been seven years since my sister decided to move to Paris. After a few degrees, a Frenchman, and a very international wedding, the gorgeous baby Rafael joined our family. As a proud auntie, I couldn't wait to kiss those edible cheeks! I was also thrilled to be back in France after a few years' absence, so I eagerly jumped on the RER to join them.

Despite being part of a Francophile family, my first impactful encounter with French culture happened in middle school when French exchange students came to stay in San Diego for two weeks. There was a cute boy (isn't there always?) named Rodolphe who, I was sure, was my soul mate. The only problem was that he didn't really speak English, and I could count up to approximately eleven in French. I resolved to be able to speak to him on the following year's exchange.

I took several summer school classes in order to ensure a spot in the class that fall. I walked into French with the campus-renowned *Madame*, excited to go beyond the "Comment-allez vous?" conversation. There was one other girl sitting in the classroom.

We made nervous small talk, waiting for the teacher and the other students to arrive. Madame walked in on the hour and immediately started speaking French. After a flurry of gorgeous sounds, she spoke English and clarified that it would be just the two of us in the class for the year. Though daunting at first, it was the best possible start to learning French.

Fast forward six months later; I was Paris-bound on my first transatlantic flight. I couldn't sleep the night before and the flight seemed eternal. I just wanted to be there already! We flew into Paris then hopped on a bus that took us down to Grenoble. I parked myself right behind the bus driver and must have used every French word I knew on that drive. The long-awaited reunion with Rodolphe finally took place, though sadly he was not the dazzling man I had built him up to be. Oh well – c'est la vie! Nothing could have brought me down during that first magical week in Grenoble.

A week after we arrived, my French host surprised me with a trip to Paris for the weekend. I stepped off the train at Gare de Lyon, eyes wide open, not wanting to miss a thing. It was magical; Paris was love at first sight: Notre Dame, the Seine, the Opera Garnier – they were the most beautiful things I had ever seen. I still remember exiting the Trocadero metro station and seeing the Eiffel Tower for the first time. It was surreal.

After graduating high school, I decided to take a gap year. I joined my sister in Paris, where we spent a year living together in a tiny apartment on the 8th floor – with no elevator, of course. It was one of the greatest years of my life. I learned what it was like to do your laundry at a Laundromat and return with the clothes by pushing a suitcase full of damp clothes up the stairs. I finally began to cook, burning both pasta and rice on my first attempts. This was the year I pushed past the limits of my little suburban bubble, traveled to England, Spain, Italy, and all over France, and decided that I would be a professional opera singer. I immersed myself in French culture and returned to California feeling like a world citizen.

I was twenty-three when I got on the flight and came back to visit my sister and new nephew and get a brief taste of Paris. In the four years that had gone by, I had returned to the US for college, earned a degree in Music and German and was ready to conquer the world. After graduation I moved to Los Angeles to study with a very renowned voice teacher and continue on the path to becoming a professional opera singer. It was the perfect next step.

Sadly, things didn't pan out the way they were supposed to. I ended up with a Craigslist roommate and her four frightening jumbo-size rabbits that owned the place. Then my voice teacher had to limit our lessons to once a month when two lessons a week are ideal. Traffic was horrific, and my savings were quickly diminishing. The LA dream had started to turn sour.

My sister offered up a new invitation to visit her in Paris; I was promptly on a plane to France for a two-week stay and a much-needed change of scenery. I called my old voice teacher at the conservatoire and scheduled a visit to see her and catch up just the day before I would return home. I decided to pack some music in my bag, just in case.

When I arrived at the conservatoire my teacher was on the phone with a student. She waved me in, smiling, and upon hanging up told me that the student who was to have her lesson at noon had just called to cancel. She asked, "Do you want a voice lesson?"

After the hour lesson we paused to chat. It felt as if no time had passed. She asked me what I was doing in the US. I rapid-fire explained that I honestly had no idea what I was doing. She paused, looking at me for a long time. "I have one spot left in my studio. Do you want it?" I immediately answered, "Yes."

Studying voice with this incredible teacher again, being back in France, starting anew, traveling through Europe - everything about this decision reverberated "yes!" I wanted Paris again.

One month and a student visa later, I was back on a plane to Paris with two suitcases, one filled with clothes and the other with music books. Rooming with my one-year old nephew for a few weeks was fun; I would wake up in a shower of toys, the smiley baby giggling in his crib. My sister and I scoured apartment ads and quickly found a newly remodeled *chambre de bonne* a five-minute walk away from her place, which was later dubbed my 'tree house'.

On the top floor of a seven-story building, I spent my first year here living in a 9.5 meters squared apartment. I had a shower stall in one quarter, a corner "kitchen" (read: two hot plates, a sink, and a mini-fridge), a corner desk, a skinny armoire, and the tiniest single bed that folded in three. That was the grand tour. Where was the toilet? On the landing – shared with two other people.

Despite the lack of space and the bathroom-sharing, the year I spent in the tree house was a happy one. My voice began to improve and mature once I began working with my current voice teacher again. Her teaching method resonates with me and has shaped my voice in ways that I can't even begin to thank her for. Though the path to becoming an opera singer is hard work, I look forward to what the future will bring.

Also during this year in my little room, I took a semester-long Masters prep course at the *Sorbonne* and was later accepted to study a Masters in musicology there; and it was in the little treehouse that I started my blog, *PatriciaParisienne*.

I decided to start a blog to share my pictures and experiences in Paris. There were so many adventures and discoveries that I was making; I wanted to document them all. The easiest way was to blog. I chose PatriciaParisienne because in French, I go by Patricia, simply because Tricia doesn't exist in French. Patricia is a Latin name, albeit an older generation name, but sounds beautiful in French. I also have an irrational love of alliteration, so Patricia and Paris seemed to go hand in hand. Patricia is my French identity that is slowly but surely becoming Parisian. Voilà, *PatriciaParisienne*!

My first blog post was a review about my experience at the Paris Opera. As a mezzo-soprano, I loved being in a city with a thriving music scene and not one but two opera houses. I took advantage of the student prices and saw *The Tales of Hoffmann* by Offenbach. It was incredible! In that review I wrote about everything I thought, saw, felt, and learned and I haven't stopped writing since. I've blogged about restaurants, cafes, events in the city, fashion, museums, people, interviews; you name it. I write as often as I can because there is so much to say!

Having a blog has enabled so many things for me. I've been able to meet some wonderful people, attend some fabulous events, and see a different side of Paris that I had not even imagined. I am constantly inspired by the beauty and culture that surround me; this city is my muse. I am celebrating my one-year anniversary of the blog this January, and I am already looking forward to what the second year will bring.

I love Paris. I love that I will never run out of things to write about. There is an infinite number of places to explore. I want to share my Parisian experience with you and have you discover the French capital with me. I want you to also fall in love with the incredible City of Light.

Photo by: Claire Morris

Patricia Rosas

Mexican-American opera singer and blogger Patricia (Tricia) Rosas moved to Paris to pursue her passion for music at the Conservatoire de Paris and a master's degree at the Sorbonne. The French capital is now home, as well as her personal playground. Follow her adventures on the blog: PatriciaParisienne.com.

CHAPTER 18

Your Passion is Your Gift

Claire Morris

I remember coloring with felt tip pens. The next thing I knew I was being told by my mum that I could never play with them again. I had no idea that eating them was wrong. The news of not being able to play with them again came with much disappointment; I couldn't wait for the moment I was once again allowed to fill my books with color...

I was only two years old at that time, and you may be pleased to know, that I haven't eaten them since. However, playing with paints, pens and drawing became one of the biggest joys in my childhood. I would sit for hours and days drawing pictures and by the age of thirteen I was drawing picture perfect portraits of celebrities and family members and giving them as gifts.

I was never interested in landscapes; drawing celebrities and people I knew brought much more joy. I strived for perfection, took care in the detail and brought faces alive.

I had this "look Mum" child-like excitement. When I did a great picture I couldn't wait to show it off.

This excitement with my creations has continued through to my adulthood.

I can't wait to show my clients their pictures. I'm like, "Look at this! Come take a peek at the back of the camera, see how amazing you look." And they love to see the shots as well. When they see how good they look, it also enthuses them, they relax and we have a great time.

The first time I had a thought about photography was during my college years, in the late 90s, whilst I was studying art. A friend of mine showed me a Coke® can that she had made into a camera, I was amazed and just had to see the possibilities for myself, it was like magic.

It was the beginning of my love affair with photography. I quickly completed my art course and chose to study photography at university. I bought an old camera, built a darkroom in my bathroom, and everyone I knew became my model.

My love for live music is what inspired my early photographic career. I began photographing the live music scene in 2001 and my work soon impressed top music magazines NME and Kerrang; quickly my photos were being regularly published. I went from drawing celebrities to photographing them.

My early 20s were momentous: I had my first photographs published, I met some of my heroes and never failed to be star struck. I had Access All Areas, press passes, I was in-front of the front row, travelling around the UK photographing music artists, and it never felt like work.

Being able to combine work with play was a great achievement; as I began to be paid for my photographs I knew I would never do anything else. Being happy in a career became possible. After that, I took every step necessary to make photography my life-long career.

Over the years I progressed, learned and developed my business and myself, practicing different photographic specialisms. I opened a studio so that I could branch out into portraits and fashion. – I worked with some high-profile clients, but I always felt quite confined to a studio.

It was a portrait client who first asked me to photograph their wedding. Their booked wedding photographer had gone bankrupt, so they asked me if I'd step in on short notice and rescue them. I'd never really photographed a wedding before. Wedding photography to me always looked stiff and boring, couples stood in arches smiling awkwardly. I wanted to help them out, but I wanted to use my fashion and editorial style and do things a little differently. They were excited; and unknown to me, this was an opportunity that was about to change my life.

My romantic side won me over; I fell in love with their photographs and with weddings. The whole day was amazing, emotional, and fun. At weddings, I'm photographing people on the happiest day of their lives and that energy radiates into me.

Lifting the new wedding business off the ground took lots of hard work, and in between all this I qualified as a photography teacher. Teaching was an amazing experience for me; I loved to be surrounded by like-minded dreamers. Inspiring and motivating so many to make their passions into a business enabled me to follow my own dreams.

So you may be wondering, "Why Paris?" I can do my work wherever I want so why would I choose Paris?

It's such a beautiful city and where better than Paris to inspire my creativity. My mum began teaching me French when I was around six, so by the time I hit French classes in school I already had a good start. I was good at French in school, and because of that I received positive feedback from teachers, which made me feel good and fall in love with the language.

My parents took me to France a lot. I adored it: the way of life, trying to speak the language, the hot summers, the food and wine. I have dreamed of moving to France, particularly Paris, for a long, long time. I just never thought I actually would!

There came a time in my life when I felt I needed a new challenge. Life wasn't really moving anywhere, business was nice and steady but personally I was bored and uninspired.

Just as I began to feel this emptiness a random opportunity came up, out of the blue, at that exact moment. A friend told me he was going to rent out his place in Paris for a few months while he was travelling. We talked about many other things, as we normally did, and we hung up. Then I had a moment of realization. I thought, "It's now or never." Literally as soon as I hung up, I was ringing back, snapping up the opportunity to rent his place.

With only a basic knowledge of French, I began packing, excited for this to be the start of my new life. Within two weeks I had sold almost everything I owned and started towards moving to Paris.

There were times when I would think to myself, "Oh, maybe this is a bad idea, what on earth am I doing?" But then as I analyzed the situation, I realized, "Hang on a minute, jump forward ten years, would I regret not taking this opportunity? This might be the only one I ever have".

So here I am. Being in Paris is beyond my dreams, beyond my expectations. I daily thank my past self for taking that risk, that leap of faith. When I arrived here I just saw it as, "I have to make this work now" and I did everything within my power to do that. I just powered in and made it work, made it happen. I've made some amazing friends who are all very supportive and my French is improving with practice.

Running my own business has been amazing but also far from easy, and there have been quite a lot of obstacles along the way. It's been really hard work to get to this point. There have been times of financial despair, buckets of tears and wondering why I chose such a hard path to walk. At times I wished I had chosen to get a 'real job' so I would have had money and an easier life like my friends seemed to have. Running a business and following your passions are two completely different ball games, I've made a lot of mistakes but learning from them has been important for business and personal growth. Relationships and my social life have suffered and on top of that, at times it felt as if no one supported or believed in me. But it's the passion for what you love doing that keeps you going. If you want an extraordinary life, you have to put in extraordinary effort.

When I'm taking gorgeous romantic photographs at the Eiffel Tower at sunrise when the streets are empty or having a picnic with friends beside the Seine in summer, I have to nip myself to check that it's all real. It's like "Gosh, I'm living my dream. Wow!" You forget all the obstacles. You forget just how hard the journey has been. You realize every little struggle and obstacle suffered wasn't without reward.

I now spend my time between France and the UK and call both Paris and Yorkshire my home. There are not many people who get out of bed totally excited about work, the way I do. I know that I am very lucky. I can be based anywhere in the world and work doing what I love. It's like doing my hobby every day while making other people happy.

As I review my life up until now, if I could share one message it would be never stop dreaming. If you are really passionate about what you do, this is your gift. This gift will carry you through life. If it's a case of risking everything to achieve your dreams ask yourself, "Will I regret not doing it?" because the answer will always be, "Yes, you will regret not doing it".

Take a leap of faith, and with passion you cannot fail.

Photo by: Patricia Rosas

Claire Morris

Claire Morris based in Paris, is a British Wedding & Portrait Photographer. With 15 years experience she brings a creative, natural and editorial feel to every wedding she shoots. Her breath-taking photographs, passion and great enthusiasm for her work, have just won her a place as a finalist for the national 'Wedding Photographer of the Year 2014" award. For more information, Contact Claire at: Claire@ clairemorrisphotography.com or www.clairemorrisphotography.com

CHAPTER 19

If I Can Make It There...

Sabrina Makar

I will always remember the day I fell in love with Paris. I was just six years old and I was on a four-day trip with my parents and my sister to the capital of France. We were stuck in traffic on the quai d'Orsay between Invalides and the Alexandre III bridge and I remember thinking that the city was so beautiful and that it was where a wanted to live when I was older. One short year later I decided I wanted to be a fashion designer when I grew up. That was it! By the age of seven I knew that my destiny was in Paris.

As a teenager I couldn't wait to move to my dream city and to go to fashion school. Being raised in a place that I disliked more than anything and having a disdain for school made those years seem twice as long as they were. When I finished high school, I thought that three months later I would be living in Paris – but that was without considering the will of my parents who told me I had to learn English. They always said: "Speaking English is an absolute necessity". I must admit that they were right on that one.

So I moved to the United States. My parents would have preferred the United Kingdom but for me it was either the USA or going right away to Paris. I would not accept any other possibility.

I stayed in the States for a year and began studying fashion design. What a great year! All the people I met there were open-minded, friendly and helpful. The teachers were far different from those I had known until then. They were more like advisers who would explain all the different ways of making things and would then let me choose the one that suited me, rather than forcing me to do things the way they were personally used to. And for the first time in my life I had good friends.

I was right. Being a fashion designer was the perfect path for me. The place where I was raised and the school I went to as a young girl were not right for me. This new life felt much better. Paris was going to be the next part of my journey.

Eleven years after I had fallen in love with Paris I finally moved there. I found a lovely apartment in a typical Parisian-style building. It was small but had a beautiful fireplace, big windows, magnificent ornate moldings and was located in one of the most coveted areas of the city, between the Musée d'Orsay and Saint-Germain-des-Prés.

My dream life was off to a great start.

The dream collapsed, though, faster than I ever thought something could fall apart. To be realistic, the first weeks in a new town are never heaven: you need to furnish your home, deal with administrative tasks, discover the neighborhood and get familiar with how things run. If you are lucky, you just may make some new friends if you don't already know anyone there, which fortunately I did. But all those things, even though time and energy consuming, were not really big problems.

The first disappointment came from college. After my great freshman year in the United States, studying in Paris felt like being back in high school. Teachers were teachers and not advisers. All of the things I had learned in the U.S. were all of a sudden wrong. For example, garments made the American way were considered to be incorrect and it could only be right if something was made the French way. Even designing and styling had to measure up to the professors' tastes. Students were split in two groups: the foreigners who were all fluent in English no matter where they were from, but who could barely speak French; and the French who could barely speak English. Being able to speak both I didn't really fit in either group, making me feel even more like an outsider.

The next year I transferred to a different college. I had heard about one that was teaching haute couture and enrolled there. Unfortunately, at the time I studied there, haute couture had not been revolutionized yet by the famous designers and my avant-garde style was not well appreciated.

So I transferred once again. This third college was still not the right one but I stayed. First, I did not want to have to try all of the colleges of Paris and secondly, I realized that I had never been much of a school person. Studying was just a practical necessity for getting a job as a fashion designer; it certainly was not a high point in my life.

Despite all of this, my college years were great. I was going out to the fanciest night clubs, meeting new people all the time, enjoying days at friends' country houses, seeing beautiful museums and exhibits and, of course, shopping. On top of that I had opportunities to intern at big fashion houses, which gave me the motivation to keep studying.

Unfortunately good internships do not guarantee a job in France. It seemed that fashion designers were not considered important enough to be hired and that the job could easily be done by interns. I could probably have spent years being an intern in all the fashion houses of Paris without ever getting a proper contract.

I had no solution to change the system so I decided to change the city and move to New York.

I didn't really know where to start until I saw an advertisement in a newspaper: a six-month contract for flight attendants to fly only on the Geneva-New York route. "This is no coincidence," I thought, "this job is for me!" Most people were really surprised when I announced what I was going to do and didn't take me seriously:

"You??? A flight attendant?????"

"You??? Wearing an awful, oversized, shoulder-padded navy blue uniform?????? You always said that you would never do a job in uniform!"

Well, never say never.

Two months later I was a flight attendant. Four months after that, September 11th happened. The company went bankrupt and I was dismissed.

But the passion for travel was in me and even though I always knew that I would go back to fashion one day, I decided to be a professional traveler for a while.

One of the greatest advantages of being a flight attendant is that you don't drive or take public transportation to go to work, you fly. Based in Zurich, living in Paris. Based in London, living in Paris. Things started to be more complicated when I started to work in business jets. As a VVIP flight attendant, you don't pay for your tickets to join the aircraft base, the company does. And they will pay any price to make sure that you are there on time. But even a first class seat won't get you there if the air traffic controllers or others are on strike and therefore they don't take flight attendants who live in France! After having applied to every company I could find, I used someone's address in Switzerland. I got a call the very next day.

One month later the financial crisis started worldwide and companies weren't recruiting anymore. After a year of freelancing I realized it was time to go back to my dream of a career in design.

As soon as I said that I was setting up my own fashion company, everybody told me that I should leave Paris. Too many administrative papers, too many taxes. I came to Paris, the capital of fashion, because I wanted to be a fashion designer running my own company and now that I was about to do it, I should leave? How ironic!

The road might not have been exactly what I wanted or expected. Paris is probably one of the toughest cities to live in. And even though I sometimes have a love/hate relationship with it, every time I am away for a long time, I miss it. So I was not going to leave. And I probably never will – at least never completely.

Paris is the city I dreamed of as a little girl and though my path has taken me in different directions than I had imagined when I was a seven-year-old, this is where I finally established my fashion design company. And it feels wonderful to know that despite the obstacles along the way, what I knew I would do with my life is a reality. Funny how all the pieces end up coming together!

Paris, if I can make it here, I'll make it anywhere!

Photo by: Claire Morris

Sabrina Makar

Sabrina Makar is a fashion designer and entrepreneur based in Paris. Always working on multiple projects, she is the founder and owner of the label SABRINA MAKAR and of Squares & Circles, a multi-brand e-shop that gathers designers from all over the world. To learn more about her work, go to www.sabrinamakar.com and www.squares-circles.com

======================== CHAPTER 20

I was Born in Paris

Sonia Hadjadj

I was born in Paris, in a hospital near Notre-Dame-de-Paris. Although my parents loved the Parisian lifestyle, they thought it would be best for my siblings and I to grow up in a southern suburb of Paris, where we could have a garden and enjoy quality family time visiting the Château de Vaux-le-Vicomte and Château de Fontainebleau, castles which were close to where they established our home.

Living in the suburbs isn't as reclusive as some people may lead you to believe. To go and see movies with my friends in the capital (the only place that showed – and still does – films in their original version), I only had to jump into a train that would take me to the center of Paris in fifty minutes. Thinking about it, as a child and as a teenager, I had the best of both worlds: the peace and quiet of a Wisteria Lane-like neighborhood and the excitement of Paris so easily in reach.

I did part of my law studies near my hometown and the other half in Paris, near the Jardin du Luxembourg. In France you sign up for at least 5 years of studying law after getting your *baccalauréat*; then in order to become a lawyer you also have to pass the Bar exam. I succeeded and went on to study for almost two additional years at the Bar School in Versailles.

During that time, I continued to take courses and, most importantly, was an intern in law firms. The hours were very intense, almost insane. But it was 2008, a time when internships were difficult to find; so I was willing to work hard and I was even grateful to be able to prove myself in a business environment.

A fan of Kate Bush, Pink Floyd and American movies such as *Birdy* and *Ferris Bueller's Day Off*, I dreamt of living in an English speaking country like the United States or England where all my cultural references came from. Several of my friends who had enrolled in business school were living abroad, some in India, others in Asia, while a few had the chance to do an Erasmus year in Europe (the Erasmus exchange program allows European students to study in the European university of their choice without having to pay the tuition fees).

I myself finally got to experience the working abroad experience when I was hired by a company in Dublin (Ireland) for six-months as part of my training for the Bar. It deeply changed me. I did not know anyone in Dublin when I got there, except for one French girl with whom I shared a common friend but whom I had never met before. She turned out to be of great help to me, helping me figure out basic things like how to get an Irish phone number.

I was working in a subsidiary of a global French corporation where I ended up handling all the legal work alone. I reported to the Finance Director, an extraordinary woman and manager who influenced me tremendously. Great responsibilities were entrusted to me within the first weeks. It was quite a challenge. I had to study Irish law – which is common law based, while French law is civil law based – and deliver the work at the same time. Getting used to the Irish accent was also challenging: in the beginning, even buying a ticket for the bus worried me!

I learned a lot about Irish culture but perhaps most importantly about myself: my abilities, my strengths and my limits. Thanks to this job and my living abroad experience, I developed a self-confidence I never thought I had in me.

I had to come back to Paris to complete the Bar qualifications with a final internship here. It was really difficult for me to leave Dublin to work in a French environment again: mindsets are so different from the ones in Ireland and I found myself being given little responsibility and feeling barely involved. I knew it would be tough and stressful to work in Paris but I did not expect to be so disappointed. Missing Dublin too much, I moved back there and got my old position back after obtaining the Bar certificate.

Picking up my work where I had left it, I stayed for a couple of years, during which time I was introduced to the company's legal team in England, based in London, and got to work closely with them. It was nice and stimulating to receive support from fellow legal colleagues.

Love brought me back to Paris and I started practicing law within a law firm. As had happened previously, I was confined to uninteresting tasks with no client contact whatsoever. To be blunt, it was boring. Add to that the long hours and pressure – I felt like a robot. I was not allowed to bring in my experience and expertise, let alone my personality. I could picture myself in five years in the same position, which was really depressing. This year and a half was a real struggle that led me to conclude that I did not fit in with that system.

Talking with other former expats who had come back to live in France as well, I realized I was not the only one feeling that same kind of "blues". Most of us – we were all within the same age group, mid-twenties/early thirties – wanted to fly away abroad again as soon as possible. We just felt there were opportunities elsewhere that we simply couldn't encounter in France.

After some time – and a burnout – I decided to truly think about what I wanted out of my life. I had always been a good, hard-working student, intern and lawyer. It became clear to me that I did not feel content and happy with myself, as I thought I would after so many years of intense studying.

The disillusion hit me hard: reality was nothing like I was told it would be growing up. The formula "work your ass off + be a good girl + pile up prestigious internships" did not equal a dream job and great income. I did not have either of them. Worse, I was stressed from the moment I woke up to the moment I went to bed. I did not eat well, I did not sleep well and I did not, of course, have much time left to spend with my family, friends and boyfriend. Making so many sacrifices to barely make ends meet was absurd. I know most people don't buy that lawyers are not all filthy rich but it's the naked truth: a lot of us struggle financially.

What I wanted was simply to make a decent living, to be able to support myself and to travel the world. So I quit my job, read blogs, articles and books to find out how others were turning their dreams into reality. Tim Ferris' book *The 4-Hour Workweek* was a revelation and I also got great insights from talking with a young lawyer overseas who had made the leap of going solo to achieve a different lifestyle, away from the rat race they would have had to put themselves through to work in a big firm.

If they found the courage to step out of the crowd, it's because they had asked themselves this very simple question: "Whose expectations am I trying to fulfill?" I had always wanted to work on my own for the independence and freedom it gives. It was the reason I went to law school in the first place. But I lost that vision along the way as the system forced into my brain this idea that I must follow the same path as everyone else if I didn't want to fail.

What stopped me from bailing on this system of terror was one thing: fear. Lots of fears actually: fear of judgment, fear of failing, fear of making the wrong choice... When I realized I was slaving away to fulfill someone else's expectations, I finally found the strength to end my misery and to start my own solo practice.

At a Meetup event in Paris, I met amazing expat ladies: our conversations alone inspired me for days. I had a strong feeling I had to find a way to work with them. Still missing the Anglo-Saxon spirit, I decided to specialize in helping expatriates set up and run their businesses in Paris.

Taking this leap of faith, going solo in Paris with no clients, is the best decision I have ever made! Everyone has to define what happiness consists of for them; for me it is freedom – the right to manage my time the way I want to in order to make my dreams come true. Now that I have changed my view on my work and myself, I see Paris differently, too, and I have come to love it. I have met wonderful, dynamic, entrepreneurial people here who amaze me with their energy and their ideas on how to do business differently. I allow myself more time to be with my friends, to go to the theater and to rugby games.

I have learned that success depends little on where you are but rather a lot on doing what you love. When you do something you're passionate about, your imagination runs free and you come up with ideas that will surprise even you.

Photo by: Claire Morris

Sonia Hadjadj

Sonia Hadjadj is a French bilingual business lawyer who works with entrepreneurs and business owners helping them create or grow their companies. Whether you want to launch a tour guide business in Paris, a technology start-up or expand your existing business to France and Europe, Sonia is here to assist through all the steps and make sure your business stays protected. When not helping entrepreneurs bring their vision to life, Sonia loves watching sci-fi movies and series, practicing her yoga or planning her next travel trip. You can connect with Sonia by email info@yourfrenchbizlawyer.com, twitter @sonia_hdj and on her website www.yourfrenchbizlawyer.com

There's Never a Wrong Time
Yulin Lee

How we got to Paris was the sheer result of an open mind. It's that simple! By chance, my husband learned of an opportunity to work in the Paris office of his company. When the possibility came to us, it felt like a dream, too good to be true. Instead of waking up from the dream by telling ourselves, "It would be really nice, but…", we decided to carry on with that dream by making it a reality.

We were living in Palo Alto, California, in the heart of Silicon Valley and the hub of technology. With my husband in the technology sector and me in real estate and finance we were living a fast-paced life, chasing the American dream like everyone else, while unconsciously sinking deep into a comfort zone and material burdens. With both sets of our families around, many friends, and lots of enriching activities for the children, life was good, with the California sunshine to top it all off. It was hard to imagine why we would want to change it all. That was a question our family asked us and one that we discussed ourselves into the wee hours of the night.

We certainly had our moments of doubt. What kind of school would we put our children in? What about *my* career? Oh, and the fact that none of us spoke French certainly added more weight to the daunting prospect of having to adjust to a new country and culture. Despite all the "what about this" and "what about that" questions, my husband and I shared the same sentiment that it would be a good adventure to get us out of the rat race and try a new and different lifestyle.

On the day, four months later, when the Pods truck loaded up all of our worldly possessions, I felt a sudden sensation of lightness. I wonder if that's how snakes feel when they shed their skin for new growth.

Now that we are happily settling into our third year in Paris, I can personally testify that the amazing and enriching experience of learning and living in a different culture outweighs any justifications for "why we couldn't do it at this time." There is no better time, nor is there a wrong time. The "right" time is NOW, for any ambition you may have. We can reminisce about the past and hope for the future, but the present is the only thing that's real. If we hadn't jumped on this opportunity, we would still be living in the comfort of our old home and lifestyle *wishing* that, one day, we could live abroad and "do something different".

"Quel est votre origin?"

I have never been reminded of my Chinese origin as much as I have since moving to Paris. Although I was born and raised in China, my thirty years of living in California has made me an "American" in many ways. I speak fluent Chinese, but I think in English. Most of my lifestyle choices are "American", but I still carry certain Chinese values deep within. Although I myself have had many lapses and crises of identity, most people in California don't typically drill me on where I was born or whether I was Chinese or Japanese or whatever. Either people really don't care, or it's a result of social conditioning in political correctness.

One thing I have learned about the French culture is that French people pay great attention to your "origin". After two years plus, we can now accurately predict how a conversation with a stranger would unfold. It goes something like this:

A French person: "where are you from?" or "what's your nationality?"

Us: "we are from California" or "we are Americans."

The French person: "Ah, oui, but really, where are you originally from?" (with emphasis on "originally")

Us: "Well, I was born in China, my husband is from Hong Kong, and our children were born in America".

The French person: "Ah, so you are Chinese".

These exchanges have been particularly interesting for our children. Having been born and then starting to grow up in the American melting pot, they haven't really had to face the question of "who am I?" until now. It has forced them to recognize their ethnic heritage. As an old Chinese saying goes: "never forget your roots". I am sure my ancestors are thanking the French from above right now. To our amusement, our daughter has now perfected her answer: "I'm a Chinese descendant born in America, but live in Paris and love Japanese sushi and wish to learn to speak Greek." Now, how many more cultures can we add to that statement has become one of our family challenge games.

During my younger years, I used to get the same, "Where are you from?" question, mostly as a pickup line – the poor souls didn't know that it was *the* turnoff for me. Irritated, my standard answer was, "I'm from Mars".

Fast forward to the present, I've decided to spare my French fellows my story of being a Martian. I also learned through reading *Sixty Million Frenchmen Can't Be Wrong* by Jean-Benoît Nadeau that the French culture does place a great deal of emphasis on their origin. To them, it *is* what defines who you are.

It's actually not surprising. In America we value individuality, and that's how we teach our children: "Be yourself!" Naturally, we want others to see us for who we are as an individual. In France, as we have learned through our experiences in the local school, kids are taught and trained to conform. Without the mentality of individuality, people relate to each other by assessing which "group" or "origin" you are from, whether it's socially, demographically or ethnically.

Re-Inventing Yourself Is Not a Luxury, But a Necessity

This question of origin has made me look deeper within myself to reflect on who I really am, and in an unexpected way, also made me explore what I can become. My life in Paris so far can be characterized as living outside the box; a box that was previously defined by complete incompetence in the kitchen, total hopelessness in any manual craft work, and a lack of patience for fine arts. Before Paris, I had been leading a typical Silicon Valley fast-paced life with no time to stop and smell the roses.

Like most francophiles who move to Paris, I watched the movie *Julie & Julia* right after we arrived, but I had no illusions about becoming the next Julia Child. However, I have managed to surprise myself with the fact that on most evenings, I typically spend about two hours preparing dinner. It started out as a necessity for me to enter the kitchen since I'm the one who is not working, but then, without my knowing it, the soothing rhythm of washing, cutting and preparing the food grew on me. This is something that I would have never imagined possible for me. I marvel at the irony of me learning to make a Thanksgiving turkey and stuffing in Paris, and it brings a smile to my face. Not only can I now make a dinner with a sense of ease, I have also discovered imagination and creativity which I never thought I had.

My adventures in the kitchen have given me the confidence to explore the other incompetent sides of me. A year ago, taking a tip from a friend, I enrolled myself in a *cartonnage* class. Cartonnage is a traditional craft of making embellished objects from thick cartons and decorated with beautiful paper or fabric. Once a week, I drag myself through the Metro with a boat-sized bag filled with supplies and tools, to arrive at a classroom with a handful of French ladies whose company I enjoy immensely. During these classes, I will myself to work with my hands, and struggle with precision. While the craft work is challenging, my consolation prize is the chance to listen in on the Paris gossip in French, and sometimes even participate a little with my broken French. This is a huge step up from my usual shameless eavesdropping in the Metro, a "game" that I like to play to see how many French words I can catch in a random conversation.

I have never been much of a museum buff but what Paris has afforded me is the luxury of combining my passion for reading biographies about historical figures with easy access to museums where many of these historical figures came to live. Musée D'Orsay is one of my favorite hangout spots, initially because of its architecture. However, now that I have had the time to read about the impressionists, their private lives and the era in which they lived, each of those paintings becomes more vivid and memorable. My interest in learning more about arts and history grew as I paid homage to all the wonderful museums and exhibits that take place in Paris each year.

As I reflect on each one of these new personal frontiers that I have embarked on since arriving in Paris, as minor as they may seem individually, I realize that the aggregate effects on me as a person who aspires to grow has been tremendous. Through these seemingly mundane activities, I have been building mental muscles for stretching out of my comfort zone. I believe that it is these mental muscles that will help me stay relevant and engaging in this fast-changing world. My goal in life is to keep re-inventing myself and stay a perpetual learner, and what better place to start that journey than in Paris?

Photo: Author's personal collection

Yulin Lee

With a Computer Science degree and a MBA, for 12 years, Yulin worked for companies like Microsoft and Adobe, as a Marketing Manager. But her real passion is helping people in RE investments and financial management, which she had done for 10 years before moving to Paris. She now has a private practice as a Financial Coach, helping women achieve financial independence through positive mindset, healthy money habits, and rigorous planning. www. yulinlee.com

CHAPTER 22

Brave Heart

Margot Nightingale

"Putain, on meurt vite !"
Damn, you die fast!

-- Husband's first words upon waking up from coma

Frozen

The short-lived but biting cold front that seized Western Europe in February 2012 left a deeper scar of frostbite on our family than we could have imagined that winter. As the good citizens of Paris were suffering from a *froid de gueux* that sent them scurrying for shelter inside warm cafés and bars, the same frigid wind tossed my family headfirst across a frozen landscape fit only for a warrior with a fierce will to live.

Monday morning, 6th February. A steamy hot coffee was mandatory to start the day, in order to warm chilled hands and fuel the body. Down the street from my son's school in the family-friendly 15th arrondissement, I met up with two friends at our regular neighborhood café, Cosmos. Blissfully unaware that just a few streets

away on a Roland Garros-red tennis court, seven stories ι
events were unfolding with my husband's health. My frien
enjoyed our warm drinks and chatted away insouciantly about the
latest twists and turns in the French Presidential election and the
obstinately cold temperatures outside. I was soaking up that bonding
feeling that occurs when you take a moment for yourself after key
morning tasks are completed.

Normal protocol was broken, however, by the fact that I didn't
have my cell phone with me that morning. Forgetting to charge it the
night before, it was left at home next to my bed.

At the café, conversation soon turned to chicken soup. A collective
decision was made that we were craving it and should all make it
for dinner that night. Breaking normal protocol yet again, instead of
returning straight home to change and go to work, we three ambled
down the rue du Commerce in hopes of finding an open butcher
to buy the star of the show, the *poulet*. (Many Parisian butchers are
closed Mondays after staying open to serve customers over the busy
weekend for Sunday *dejeuner en famille* where fresh roast is *de rigueur*.)

My friends and I were making the queue at the rotisserie stand
inside *Monoprix* (a French supermarket chain, as we had no luck
finding an open butcher shop) when I suddenly felt a shudder and in
my head I re-played Henry's voice from the earlier darkness of that
morning. "Margot, it's 6:30." Then he was off, a quiet figure in the dark
holding a tennis racquet and dressed in white like a ghost.

Bypass

His was the scary scene you hear about but never want to receive
news has actually happened. No mention of any pain, no sweating,
no nausea or breathy pleas for a glass of water. Instead, his day went
like this: regular tennis game with the regular group of guys at
7:00am, massive heart attack a half hour in, collapse in cardiac arrest,
life-saving CPR administered by one of his brave tennis partners,
emergency quadruple bypass surgery an hour later.

By dinnertime: hanging on by a thread.

The surgeon on duty that morning confessed later that he figured Henry had less than a 20% chance of pulling through the surgery, given the massive blockages that were strangling his heart. But to work he went, and with his skilled craftsmanship, he saved my husband's life.

Across the universe

"I just wish he'd given us a bit more warning," is the laconic re-tell from the other man who saved Henry's life that morning. Sudden-death cardiac arrest of his backhand partner was not a game play that Mike L. had prepared to tackle that morning on the tennis court. A retired researcher who spent most of his career at UNESCO in Paris, Mike had taken a CPR course at the local mayor's office (every Parisian neighborhood has one) four years earlier with his 23-year-old daughter. They participated in the course because they thought it would be a useful life skill to learn.

Like so many graduates of the course, he had never found himself in a position where his training would be tested. On the morning of 6th February, he barely remembered what to do first, but the miracle is that he didn't waste a second questioning it, instead falling to his knees to get to work.

Mike's wife, a sweet-voiced Burmese UNESCO retiree, became a reassuring support through our telephone conversations that followed in the days to come, sharing news of Henry's progress. I'm still convinced she is a peaceful Buddhist monk in a flowing orange sari, disguised as earthly Rita.

She gave me strength to continue talking to Henry when I felt my energy waning or hope slipping. Henry was in a coma, and he was showing no signs of wanting to come out of it.

Rita reminded me that wherever he was in the universe, he was all by himself and might be scared. So I talked to him as I sat by his bedside. I kept the conversation going as my hand rested on his arm, stroking it lightly from his elbow to the tips of his fingers, the only portion of his body not strangled by tangled wires and IVs. I read to him. Beaudelaire's *Alchemy of Sorrow* and Thomas Hardy's *Far from the Madding Crowd.*

Our son Martin squeezed his arm and whispered to him. He was brave and I never saw a tear fall from his eye. But Henry didn't make a move. He was frozen, across the universe.

The silence of angels

My biggest enemy during those days of waiting (hoping) for Henry to wake up was fatigue, combined with a Mike Tyson-type punch to the stomach. I knew I had to stay afloat, for the sake of my son.

Earlier I had discouraged friends and family from jumping on a plane and coming over to be with me, which many kindly offered to do. I felt an indescribable yearning to be a small army of just the immediate family in those first days of alarm.

Henry and I had moved to Paris two years earlier in order to spend more time with his three older sons from his first marriage, and to enroll our son in a bilingual school so he could adopt the language of his heritage. But this meant that none of my family, friends, or traditional support system were nearby now when I needed them.

There was new information pouring forth daily, in a foreign language, and decisions that would have to be made if things didn't turn out well. I couldn't even see how shut down my body was until a week into the vigil I realized I hadn't shed a tear. Tears came, finally, in spades, but devastating news can lock up the instruments, shattering us in myriad ways.

Sunday morning, six days into Henry's ordeal, I found myself in the wooden pews of the American cathedral on Paris's chic right bank. I sorely needed to find my center and steady my teetering stance. That morning I simply woke up and needed Grace.

The uplifting children's choir, where my son is a member, had top billing and would be singing all three anthems and fractions throughout the service. I maintained a vision that the angelic voices of the children would drift across the rooftops of Paris like a red balloon and wake Henry up.

As I slid into the pew near the nave and took a seat on the worn surface of the bench, I couldn't help wonder if I would be back here in a few weeks for his funeral. The doctors had begun speaking in hushed tones.

That negative thought, along with another haunting one that my husband was going to die on Valentine's Day, was thankfully my last of the ordeal. Once I was on my knees at the altar, I lifted my head toward the four bronze angels blowing their trumpets around a stained glass window. Suddenly, my universe, as small and insignificant as it was in the scheme of all the suffering and beauty in the world every day, became very still and quiet. The situation being 100% out of my control, I handed it over. And with its departure came the slow burn of a candle that would lead the way toward the light out of this crisis.

Later, as I was walking home through the *Champs de Mars* with my son in tow, my cell phone rang. "You better get down here Margot. Things are happening!" commanded the urgent voice of a friend who had generously offered to sit with Henry that morning so I could hear Martin sing. "He opened his eyes!"

Strangely, I had the same numb reaction I had when I first heard the news a week ago that he'd collapsed. Having paced the bottom of the trench for the last days, it took a moment for my mind to react. Once engaged however, we fled off in the direction of the hospital *La Pitié Salpêtrière* in the fifth arrondissement.

Indeed it was true. Henry had opened his eyes and when I leaned over him to kiss him in sheer joy, I was silenced with tears, looking into those open eyes, their unique color of light brown like an autumnal falling leaf, shining back up at me.

Margot Nightingale

Margot Nightingale is a writer and educator living in Paris. Her day job keeps her entertained and on her toes; she runs her own business helping French professionals practice and perfect their English conversation and business vocabulary. She's currently re-reading *The third man* by Graham Greene with one of her executive clients. She lives with her husband, a designer, and 10 year old son, a budding magician specializing in card tricks. www.margotnightingale.com

My Favorite Place in Paris

Mady Mendes

My favorite place in Paris is Jardin des Tuileries because it's the most beautiful place in Paris. There is a nice view of the Eiffel tower and l'Arc de triomphe. It's a very romantic place where you take a long walk with your loved one. It's a magic place where I can find peace in Paris. Jardin des Tuilerie is the heart of the city of love.

Patricia Rosas

One of my favorite places in Paris is the Opera Garnier. It's the most beautiful building in the world. I love walking up Avenue de l'Opera toward the golden angels resting on top of the columns. Day or night, it always looks stunning and illuminated. Today, it is primarily the home of the Paris Opera Ballet, or *Ballet de l'Opéra de Paris*, but you can still see a few operas a year, thankfully. Majestic, the building exudes classical Parisian elegance and glamour with its stony exterior as well as the vibrant Chagall ceilings. Palais Garnier is a true architectural masterpiece.

Sanda Taranu

I love following what I like to call "my" itinerary: starting with the amazing Gallery Vivienne (4 Rue des Petits Champs, Paris 2nd arr), down Rue de la Banque (#7) for an "out of a fairytale moment" in front the glamorous Ana Quasoar bridal couture boutique, and onto the peaceful little square, which looks removed from a southern resort, with its charming Basilique Notre Dame des Victoires. Continuing to the Christian library called Au coeur Immaculé de Marie for a good testimonial book (8 Rue des Petits Pères) and ending at the little boulangerie with art nouveau walls right next door. Just perfect.

Celine Douay

I love to walk in Montmartre at the weekend; cafés and shops are open there on Sundays. Montmartre is not only home of the Sacre Coeur Basilica, which is very beautiful; it is also a village in Paris with cobbled streets, where you can meet several kinds of artists: painters, musicians, photographers... It is a romantic corner. The walls speak of love, but not only that, rebellion and art reside there as well. I like to relax on a café terrace in this peaceful neighborhood where an intimate and romantic atmosphere is always present. Montmartre is also the place of the famous movie "Amelie". In Montmartre, I feel light and creative!

Jennifer Manson

My favorite district is the 6th arrondisment, the famous Left Bank, where philosophers Sartre and de Beauvoir drank coffee and discussed their view of life; where Hemingway strolled and Oscar Wilde died. The streets are clean here, washed by patient men with their street sweeping machines and more frequently by the spectacular Paris rain, coming fast and brief, as it so often does. I have my favorite places, my favourite pieces of art: Eugène Delaplanche's statues of Eve in the Musee d'Orsay; the Cour Marly in the Louvre with its cathedral-like whispering echoes and silvery light.

Sabrina Makar

I love to walk the streets of Paris. One of my favorite routes is from the Passerelle des Arts to the Eiffel Tower, through the streets of Saint-Germain-des-Pres. It is the area where I spent most of my time during my first years in Paris and every time I walk on the Rue de l'Université, I glance at my first apartment. Sometimes, on my way I stop at Ladurée on Rue Jacob to enjoy a cup of tea with delicious macarons in the beautiful salon on the first floor.

Françoise Bor De Ley

My favorite place in Paris is the Michelin-starred restaurant: Le Jules Verne. I like this place because my husband (re) proposed to me there after 13 years of living together. The atmosphere of this place is magical. To get there, you take the private elevator on the Eiffel Tower and then climbing to the sky begins ... As you sit at your table you can take in all of the "City of Lights"! You dine in the midst of clouds and angels. As for the food ... If you love French cuisine and enjoy the city of Paris, this stop is a must! Address: 2nd floor of the Eiffel Tower - 75007 PARIS

Sonia Hadjadj

L'ile Saint Louis, in the center of Paris and the Seine, is near to my heart. I lived my first years there and I love its atmosphere.

Rebecca Earley

People always ask me what I like most about France, and my response never changes. A fresh baguette, hot out of the oven, from your local boulangerie. My local boulangerie is right on the corner of Rue de Rennes and Rue de Mézières in the 6th arrondissement. I actually don't know its name, because the only sign outside says "boulangerie" and "pâtisserie." They are always busy, which means your chances of getting a piping hot baguette are high. Go on the greyest of Paris days, or the most beautiful days of spring, and you will always leave with a smile, remembering how much you love this city.

Michelle Pozon

I love to bike through Paris! Grey or sunny, Paris is always beautiful, even in the rain. My favorite stretch is from the Invalides, along the Pont Alexandre III, watching the clouds around the gilded statues on the bridge with the Eiffel tower to one side and the Grand and Petit Palais just up ahead.

Lesley Kirk Renaud

Angelina's tea room is really a place not to be missed after taking a stroll through the Tuileries gardens just opposite on the rue de Rivoli, Paris 1ère. You will find yourself plunged in a chic and bustling ornate tea room where you will be tempted by the array of handmade fresh cakes and pastries next to a beautiful display of fine goods to buy. You will be greeted and seated at small tables, immaculately set where you receive prompt service! Angelina's is a refined venue with a touch of the belle époque nostalgia dating back to 1903! I have had many a beautiful moment here so I recommend this lovely elegant place, a voluptuous venue between serenity and gourmet pleasure...their hot chocolate is not to be missed either!

Address: 226 rue de Rivoli – 75001 Paris

Alecia Caine

I have so many favorite places in Paris but for me, I think café life is the most Parisian experience that *j'adore*. You can find me in any number of cafés, Carette's in Trocadero or Place des Vosges, Angelina for the best hot chocolate... writing in my journal, recounting my adventures in France. But my ultimate favorite is Café Carlu in Cité de l'Architecture et du Patrimoine, in the palais de Chaillot at 1 Place du Trocadéro and 11 Novembre, in the 16th *arrondissement*. The food is great and very reasonable and I can hang out there for hours writing while gazing up at the Eiffel tower, a most inspirational view. Just being in the architecture museum is very inspiring because all the great buildings I adore started as a dream and a plan, just as I am building my life around my dream and plan.

Julia Willard

As much as I love the hustle and bustle of Paris, it is the spots for refuge from the noise and chaos that I love most. The brilliantly designed parks and gardens are what keep me sane here. Parc de Bagatelles in the Bois de Boulogne is the best place in Paris to take refuge with its magnificent rose garden and lush green open spaces. There is a small entrance fee, but absolutely worth it. Read, picnic, enjoy a concert, and stay until they kick you out. Plan your route wisely.

Olena Yashchuk Codet

My favourite place in Paris is la Place Madeleine. Why? This is a Mecca for all people who appreciate a « sweet life ». The magnificent Madeleine church is surrounded by luxury shops: La Durée is a Temple of the famous "macarons", Fauchon and Hédiard are palaces full of chocolate, fruits, cakes... everything is a real piece of art and the prices are like haute couture. Just walk five or ten minutes and you'll find Galeries Lafayette Gourmet – another "must visit" place with its fine food from all over the world. If you are not so ambitious, just walk in any nice "boulangerie" which is almost always making true French patisserie – and you won't be disappointed!

Karen Reb Rudel

My favorite place in Paris is wherever I happen to be giving a tour. I am so grateful to each and every one of my clients who always inspire and motivate me to continue sharing my stories and knowledge about this fantastic city I now call my home.

Petronela Zainuddin

I love the area of Canal Saint Martin where I live. For a creative mind, like myself, this area is full of inspiration and positive energy. During a sunny day I often walk by or have a picnic with my husband at the canal. Then we usually go to Artazart Design Bookstore for inspiration and end up eating bo bun at Le Petit Cambodge. On Sundays you can find us having gluten free brunch and divine cappuccino at Thank You My Deer.

Geneviève Prono

If you wish to find a combination of peace and beauty you must not miss the museum and the gardens of Albert Kahn in Boulogne Billancourt at the periphery of Paris. You'll find it at 10-14 rue du Port, metro Boulogne – Pont de Saint Cloud. You will travel time and continents as you go along the exhibition gallery, the old village filled with temples, lanterns, stone paths edged of the Japanese garden, the greenhouse, orchard and rose garden of the French gardens, the English gardens, on to a forest of Blue Atlas cedars and Colorado spruces and a reproduction of the Vosges Moutains forest of conifers. Before 1936, when it opened to the public, this space devoted to world peace was visited only by dignitaries including various poets, philosophers (as Tagore) and Kings.

Yulin Lee

Musee Jacquemart-Andre is my favorite place in Paris. I love the whole setting, being in a previously private residence. Each time I visit there, I can't help but to imagine what it was like to be living there. They have a great permanent collection and often have interesting temporary exhibits. I also enjoy the concerts/events that are held there throughout the year. There is a very nice café inside, a great place for afternoon tea or Sunday brunch. Address: 158 Boulevard Haussmann, 75008 Paris

Margot Nightingale

When not hopping around Paris on the *Velib* meeting clients, I love visiting my favorite galleries dotting the amazing cultural landscape of Paris. *La fondation Cartier pour l'art contemporain; La fondation Henri*

Cartier Bresson, and *La Galerie Camera Obscura* are just a few of my go-to spaces for inspiration and photography.

Dawn Z Bournand

This gorgeous city is filled with too many must-see places and can't be missed experiences to choose just one favorite so instead I chose 'one of my favorites' and a place I always recommend for visiting friends to see: Musée Rodin. The museum is located in the home where Rodin lived and created many of his great works and is one of the city's most intimately beautiful spots. With Rodin's (and Camille Claudel's – Rodin's student and lover) masterpieces placed throughout the chateau it is a perfect place to spend a rainy afternoon marveling at the beauty crafted from simple pieces of stone. If you are lucky enough to visit on a sunny day, you can also walk the lush gardens filled with rose bushes and Rodin sculptures. A perfect way to spend an afternoon in Paris!

"There is no greater agony than bearing an untold story inside you."

Maya Angelou

About the Authors

The Paris Women of Success is a network of professional women created by business and life coach Dawn Z Bournand. From this group of over 300 women, 22 bestselling authors in the making, seized the opportunity and said yes to sharing their stories with the world. These authors, businesswomen, leaders and mothers found each other in Paris as "like attracting like" does. Together they created this book to empower women and to encourage them to live their best life possible.

For more information on the My Paris Story book, the authors and upcoming events: www.myparisstory-thebook.com

Made in the USA
San Bernardino, CA
01 August 2016